3

PERSPECTIVES ON AGING AND HUMAN DEVELOPMENT Series

INSTITUTIONALIZATION AND ALTERNATIVE FUTURES

EDITOR: JON HENDRICKS

Routledge
Taylor & Francis Group
LONDON AND NEW YORK

First published 1971 by Baywood Publishing Company, Inc.

Published 2018 by Routledge
2 Park Square, Milton Park, Abingdon, Oxon, OX14 4RN
52 Vanderbilt Avenue, New York, NY 10017

First issued in hardback 2018

Routledge is an imprint of the Taylor & Francis Group, an informa business

Library of Congress Catalog Card Number: 79-65156

Library of Congress Cataloging in Publication Data

Main entry under title:

Institutionalization and alternative futures.

(Perspectives on aging and human development series ; 3)
Includes bibliographies.
1. Aged--Services for--United States--Addresses, essays, lectures. 2. Aged--United States--Social conditions--Addresses, essays, lectures. 3. Old age homes--United States--Addresses, essays, lectures. I. Hendricks, Jon, 1943- II. Series.
HV1461.I57 362.6'0979 79-65156
ISBN 0-89503-016-0

ISBN 13: 978-0-415-78531-0 (hbk)
ISBN 13: 978-0-89503-016-0 (pbk)

MIX
Paper from responsible sources
FSC™ C013985

Printed in the United Kingdom
by Henry Ling Limited

preface

Putting one of the folks in the nursing home is a prospect with which few of us are prepared to deal. No facile responsibility this; no easy answers either. The antipathy even the question generates inhibits a rational view of the issue to such an extent that much of the folklore of institutionalization is accepted as fact. Practitioners in the field of gerontologic service delivery are only beginning to provide insights; heretofore they could speak of the importance of a clean, well-lighted place but very little else. On both an individual and a societal level we have much to learn. The concerns people have over such basic facts of life as interpersonal relations, including conflict, sexual identity, death and so on are just as salient on the inside as outside. On the social plane, much remains to be discovered. Even now gerontologists have yet to direct their attention to what has been called the political economy of the nursing home industry. The implications of the shifting locus of responsibility, indeed the ideology of care, also remain largely unexplored. What the sociologists commonly term vested interests first delayed enactment of federal statutes, now delay their revision. Charges of abandonment by families and countercharges of gouging are hurled back and forth across the arena. Questions are all too maddeningly prolific. Too many nursing homes populated by too many people who should not be there? Or too few homes reserved for the affluent? Standards which are too strict or enforcement which is too lenient? Decisions too firmly entrenched in the hands of the medical sector, the proprietors, the bureaucracy? Invective is easy; resolution is not.

The problem is not going to go away; all indications suggest that the proportion of the population over age 75 is increasing rapidly. Therefore the nearly $4 billion spent annually by the government and the untold amounts coming from individuals, non-profit groups and proprietary interests for institutional support will increase almost as rapidly as the "target" age categories. The current thinking is that somewhere in the neighborhood of five percent of the people over 65 reside in some type of institutional facility on any given day. Of course, such a figure does not tell the whole story. It says nothing of how many people were institutionalized yesterday but have been released today. Like all averages, it masks the reality for those over age 75 when the rate of institutionalization approaches one-fifth. Claiming a five percent average also glosses the fact that something in excess of four-fifths of all deaths among those beyond retirement age occur in institutions. Obviously the range of the facilities involved is broad, running from domiciliary and personal care homes, with or without nursing services, to skilled nursing facilities, mental hospitals and acute care hospitals. In addition, there are retirement communities, residential hotels and other congregate housing arrangements which cater to those with less pressing needs.

The aim of this volume is not merely to recite a litany of institutional problems or to provide a sampler of research relevant to those charged with the delivery of services. We believe it more useful to offer a selection of articles which illustrate ways of maximizing choice, independence, well-being, and an avoidance of the emotional stunting which is too frequently associated with institutionalization. The first selection launching the discussion is the now classic "4% Fallacy" by Kastenbaum and Candy. Almost single-handedly, this article sensitized gerontologists to the pitfalls of cross-sectional statistics. The two essays in Part I serve to affirm the relevance of the 1978 Comprehensive Service Amendments to the Older Americans Act, which call for, among other things, the provision of personal care services fostering a maintenance of community ties in order to avoid institutionalization. Bennett is concerned with the negative impact of isolation, quite apart from one's capabilities. Bringing older people back from their social marginality intercepts what in many cases appears to be an inevitable trajectory. Barg and Hirsch report their experiences with an outreach program for low-income urban aged. Cross-generational ties, emphasizing indigenous workers, prompts involvements and an awareness among the clientele sufficient to offset many of the symptoms of ageism.

Once institutionalization does occur, how can the strengths of the elderly be safeguarded rather than assaulted? In Part II, the discussion revolves around just this question, with a number of suggestions for enhancing the quality of life for the institutionalized elderly. As Sherwood and her colleagues point out, successful adaptation – marked by improved life satisfaction – in long-term care facilities is not a result of chance. A number of previously existing factors carry over, mediating the process. Coupled with this is the fact that socialization into membership within the institution also follows definite gradations, like any rite of passage, and the beginnings of an intervention model start to emerge, as Weinstock and Bennett so cogently assert. Stimulating learning situations, characterized by supportive networks and low-risks, serve to challenge residents and inhibit the development of institutional neurosis. In Snyder's contribution to our ethnographic accounts of institutional life, the importance of social bonds is further stressed. Developing ties among residents whether they center around interaction or privacy, promotes rehabilitative coping mechanisms too often absent in the unresponsive living conditions of the majority of our institutions. Ostrander expands further the emphasis on prosthetic conditions under the rubric of "environmental analysis." As he makes clear, user-sensitive environments incorporate attention to physical, psychic and operational dimensions which reinforce the well being of the residents, helping each to discover their own particular niche in the circuit of institutional life.

Enriched surroundings are apparently potent influences insofar as quality and quantity of activities are concerned. Carp reports on two groups of elderly residents exposed to different environmental conditions. Matching personal needs to environmental resources, she was able to significantly alter the degree of expressed satisfaction. The last selection in this section focuses on an innovative type of behavior-mapping which is also indicative of how people feel about the events going on about them. Lawton, Patnaik and Kleban report that physical location and body position within a circumscribed area are neither random, nor without meaning. Recognizing the existence of such non-verbal cues as body posture is an essential element in promoting well-being.

Grappling with the realities of life is never easy, both for those who live in as well as those who work in facilities designed to assist the elderly. The dilemmas often pose painful choices. Part III addresses some of the paradoxes which emerge as client and provider participate in what may turn out to be a most trying interaction. Behavior which is felt to be simply troublesome may actually be based on phylogenetically induced needs for dignity. In the next article, Watson points out the all too human reactions few see as unwarranted, yet which reinforce negative self-concepts among the residents. Eight hours of changing soiled linen is bound to take its toll; unfortunately it becomes evident in the face-to-face interaction between staff and resident. Body image, staff status rank and styles of deportment vary widely, alternately complementing and contradicting the purposeful nature of the contact. If one end of the continuum is occupied by those who require the most elemental assistance in body hygiene, the other end is characterized by residents who may sometimes be "too competent for their own good." As Posner reminds us in her contribution, nursing homes are not usually intended for those who manage almost well enough on their own. In fact, doing so can work against the resident by prompting staff retribution. The name of the game is to act incompetent enough to remain eligible, which involves the precarious balancing of responding to treatment efforts while demonstrating a continued need for staff attention. Lastly, we look at a different kind of game, one set in a setting far removed from nursing homes, but one having many parallels across all congregate living arrangements. Marshall looks at the contractual arrangements between residents and management of a retirement village. While one side is betting on surviving long enough for a acceptable return on their purchase, the other expects a rapid turnover in order to arrange resale and an appropriate gain on their investment. Besides reminding us there are two sides to every treatment question, Marshall also notes that under the circumstances, the players may not behave as rationally as we might hope.

table of contents

PART THREE – INSTITUTIONAL DILEMMAS

chapter 1

INTRODUCTION THE 4% FALLACY: A METHODOLOGICAL AND EMPIRICAL CRITIQUE OF EXTENDED CARE FACILITY POPULATION STATISTICS*

Robert Kastenbaum
Sandra E. Candy

It is often said that only 4% or, at the most, 5% of the elderly in the United States are to be found in nursing homes and other extended care facilities. Evidence to support this statement is not lacking. Riley and Foner [1] used United States census data for 1960 to show that only 2.4% of Americans over the age of 65 were residing in homes for the aged and dependent. The percentage of institutionalized could be increased to 3.7% if other kinds of group quarters and extended care facilities are included in the total. It could be increased again to 4.8% if those in mental hospitals are also included. Population data for 1965, also summarized by Riley and Foner, yielded a similar picture. Slightly less than 4% of Americans over the age of 65 were residing in group facilities or institutions. This information is adequate for the

*A preliminary version of this paper was presented at the annual meetings of The Gerontological Society, San Juan, Puerto Rico, December 20, 1972.

purposes of the present paper, although more recent population statistics are becoming available.

Most gerontologists appear to be familiar with the figures that have been cited here. References to the 4% figure are encountered frequently in journals, books, classes, conferences, and governmental deliberations. This statistic has many implications. Perhaps the most common usage has been to emphasize the overwhelming percentage of elders who are *not* institutionalized. This, in turn, spins off other implications, for example, "Conditions may be deplorable in many extended care facilities, but it is more practical to concentrate our attention elsewhere because so few elders are institutionalized."

It seems to us that a very elementary kind of error is being perpetuated here, the sort we teach our students to avoid. Our utilization of these population statistics is often fallacious because we fail to recognize that *the data are cross-sectional*. Knowing how many elders are institutionalized at this moment, no matter how accurate a statement, does not tell us how many people will have resided in extended care facilities at some time in their lives. It does not give us the probabilities for an individual; only a series of longitudinal studies could answer that question satisfactorily.

Assume for sake of simplicity that the percentage of institutionalized elders at a particular point in time remains constant. Are we in a position to conclude that only 1 person in 25 who reaches old age will become institutionalized? We can conclude nothing of the sort. Common-sense urges that the probabilities must be higher. How *much* higher is an empirical question.

Perhaps it is sufficient just to have called attention to a popular fallacy in generalizing from population data in gerontology. However, we felt that a small exercise in the gathering of corrective data might be appropriate. A pair of small studies were conducted to satisfy our own curiosity and encourage others to carry out more extensive and sophisticated work on this problem. For those who are cost-conscious, it might be mentioned that the total budget was 25¢ (not supported by a grant).

STUDY 1

The first study was based upon the premise that if a person *died* in a nursing home or other extended care facility, then it is reasonable to conclude that he had indeed *been* there. The method was to read all the obituaries reported in the *Detroit News* ("Detroit Area Obituaries" rubric) for a one-year period (January 3, 1971-January 2, 1972). Place of death was the critical item noted, although other information was abstracted as well.

This method resulted in the identification of 1,184 deaths. Slightly more than half of this sample (52.7%) died in hospitals, according to the obituary notices. Interestingly, place of death was not specified in more than 20%

(21.79%) of the entries. Approximately 13% were reported to have died in private homes, and a little over 10% in nursing homes. About 2% died in other locations, for example, in automobile accidents.

If we eliminate obituaries that did not specify place of death, we then have 926 cases remaining. Of these, 13.3% died in nursing homes. Deaths in private homes remained slightly more common (16.4%), and hospital deaths proved even more dominant, rising to 67%.

This reduced sample thus consists of all deaths of persons over the age of 65 reported in the daily newspaper of a large metropolitan area with place of death specified. We see that more than three times as many elders died in nursing homes than are reported as existing in same by cross-sectional population counts. The discrepancy becomes even more pronounced if we compare deaths with the figures for elders said to reside only in homes for the aged and dependent. Our method of data classification seems to justify this comparison. We now find that 13.3% died where only 2.4% lived—a discrepancy ratio that approaches 6 to 1.

One of the obvious difficulties with this study was the high percentage of deaths in which place was not specified. Another difficulty was the question of possible missing cases, i.e., elders whose death may not have been reported in the form of a newspaper obituary. For these and other reasons we moved on to the second study.

STUDY II

Our premise remained the same—use the fact of death to establish place of residence. The difference was in source of information. This time we went directly to the death certificate.* Access was obtained to the microfilm records of all death certificates filed in the metropolitan Detroit area during the 1971 calendar year. These mortality records included 28,755 entries for persons aged 50 and over. This report is limited to those 65 and over, a population that numbered 20,234.

One could ask how many of these people died in a nursing home; this would not be identical with those who died in institutions of every type. We will report separately upon deaths in nursing homes, in extended care facilities of all types, and in hospitals. The focus is upon the first two categories. The first is limited strictly to those who died in a place that could be positively identified as a nursing home. The second includes nursing home deaths and adds those which occurred in other types of extended care facilities as well. If there was doubt concerning the nature of the facility, the death was not included in either of these categories. Typically, this meant recording a death

*We are grateful to the Michigan Cancer Foundation for use of their microfilm records.

in the hospital category, although the medical facility in question could perhaps be described more accurately as a nursing home with delusions of grandeur. Any errors in classification therefore should have resulted in an *under*estimation of deaths occurring in nursing homes and other extended care facilities.

Results

We find that approximately 20% of all deaths in the 65+ age range occurred in nursing homes, and approximately 24% occurred in the larger category that included all identifiable extended care facilities. The basic data are presented in Table 1.

Table 1. Place of Death for All Persons Aged 65 and Over in Metropolitan Detroit Area, 1971
N = 20, 234

Place of Death	*Number*	*% of Total*
All extended care facilities	4,796	23.70
Nursing homes only	4,099	20.02
Hospitals	12,631	62.43
Other	36	.18

Make a point-by-point comparison now with the usual cross-sectional population data. More than eight times as many elders died in nursing homes than were assumed to be living there. Six times as many people died in extended care facilities (the larger category) as the population data would have led us to believe.

Look at the same data from the perspective of the individual. When population data are used carelessly we assume that the odds of a person entering an extended care facility of some type are only 1 in 25. If we at least reasoned fallaciously with the appropriate figures, we would set the odds at about 1 in 40 for a person taking up residence in a home specifically designated for the aged and dependent. The present data offer a radically different set of odds: 1 chance in 4 of being in an extended care facility; 1 chance in 5 for a nursing home.

We should immediately acknowledge another factor that influences the data. Any person who resided in a nursing home but did not die there would not be counted among those deceased in institutions. This is an additional source of underestimation: more people have lived in nursing homes than have died there. The opposite is not true. Everybody who did expire in a nursing home was a resident, whether long or short-term.

Discovery was made of 72 documented instances in which an elderly person sustained an injury in a nursing home, was transferred to a hospital, and died soon thereafter of pneumonia, pulmonary emboli, myocardial infarction, or some other form of heart disease. These individuals obviously had been in a nursing home although they died elsewhere. How many other old men and women were transferred from nursing homes for other medical reasons, and subsequently died in the hospital? No information was available on this point, although moving out a terminally ill resident to die elsewhere is a well-known practice.

All the circumstances that affect the way in which death certificates are completed and in which this study was conducted, veer in the direction of underestimating the number of people who spend some time as a resident of a nursing home or other extended care facility.

Sex and Race

Are there differences in place of death between men and women, and between blacks and whites? Whites comprised 87% of the total sample, blacks 13%. There was a slight predominance of males over females: 53%/47%. The ratio of men to women was approximately the same for blacks and whites; there were about seven male deaths for every six female deaths in both samples. Data on sex and race are presented in Table 2.

Table 2. Place of Death by Sex and Race for Persons Aged 65 and Over in Metropolitan Detroit Area, 1971

Group	*Total*	*Extended care facility*	*Hospital*	*Private home*	*Other*
Women	9,541	2,789	5,350	1,305	7
Black	1,197	325	709	161	2
White	8,245	2,463	4,634	1,143	5
Other	9	1	7	1	0
Men	10,761	2,004	7,272	1,456	29
Black	1,398	277	943	170	8
White	9,363	1,727	6,329	1,286	21
Other	22	3	9	10	0
Black	2,595	602	1,652	331	10
White	17,608	4,190	10,963	2,429	26

It is clear that place of death was not equally distributed by sex. Males were underrepresented in nursing home and extended care facilities, and overrepresented in deaths recorded in hospitals and private homes. More women (58%) than men (42%) died in nursing homes, a difference of 23% from statistical expectations. This finding will not surprise those who are familiar with geriatric institutions. We would like to emphasize, however, that the present data do not include information on length of residence. We cannot say that the observed differences are related entirely to the predominance of female admissions to nursing homes. It could be that more men than women are removed from nursing homes to die elsewhere.

There is another finding that is worth pausing over. Of more than 20,000 deaths, only 36 were listed as occurring in some place other than an extended care facility, hospital, or private home. It is striking that 29 of these fatalities (about 80%) involved males. We have the impression that most of these deaths were sudden or traumatic, but our information is not complete.

The picture is quite different for race. The percentage of blacks in each of the major place-of-death categories was close to the total percentage of blacks in the study population. Remembering that 13% of all deaths in this sample involved black elders, we find 12.6% in nursing homes, 13% in hospitals, and 12% in private homes. There was a difference, however, in the fractional category of "other" deaths: here 10 of the 36 fatalities, about 28%, were black.

It remains to examine sex-by-race combinations. The tendency for a higher percentage of the women to die in nursing homes was approximately equal for both blacks and whites. There were no instances in which the relative proportion of deaths by sex was reversed for blacks and whites. On the basis of the death certificate information, then, sex appears to be a more differentiating variable than race.

Discussion

If we are concerned about "death with dignity," to use the now-popular phrase, then perhaps the hospital should be our primary concern. Almost two out of every three deceased elders (62.4%) in the metropolitan Detroit area died in a hospital. (In all, 86% died in some kind of institution.) However, there is also much reason to be concerned about the nursing home as a final environment. We have seen that approximately one elder in four dies in an extended care facility, the odds being slightly higher for women. How many of these facilities are equipped to provide physical, social, and emotional comfort to the terminally ill old man or woman? Whether we choose to emphasize quality or duration of life for the terminally ill person, it is highly doubtful that nursing homes are providing adequate services for either goal.

Many old people die in nursing homes and other extended care facilities. In the Detroit metropolitan area alone, no fewer than 336 and as many as 476 men and women died *every month* during 1971. Yet relatively little attention is given, even by nursing home activists, to improving the quality of terminal care. Federal and local governments have also been remiss.* Governmental policies and practices have done little to encourage minimally acceptable care within institutions. This failing is all the more unfortunate in view of a similar lack of attention to the development of realistic alternatives to the nursing home as a final environment.

The reluctance to become involved in terminal care and the 4% fallacy, tend to fuel each other. Dying is so unimportant or unworthy that a person should not really be counted as "living" in an extended care facility if he is in a process of terminal decline. Similarly, the misleading usage of extended care facility population statistics tends to draw attention away from the fact that many of our elders end their lives among strangers in an environment that offers little true "nursing" and scarcely resembles a "home." Perhaps abandonment of the 4% fallacy will also contribute to the abandonment of destructive attitudes and practices [2, 3].

The most general implication of this study is its reinforcement of every problem that gerontologists have already identified in the nursing home. All the painful shortcomings of the inadequate extended care facility must be regarded as of even greater consequence than previously noted. This statement perhaps should be amended to: of greater *social* consequence. Despair and indignity are as real if only one person is affected. We have known that many thousands are affected. And now we must face the fact that the true extent of the institutional care problem is of greater magnitude than usually assumed. To look at the same facts from a brighter perspective, every action that is taken to improve the quality of life in extended care facilities will be a blessing to a very considerable number of our fellow citizens.

We hope that the 4% fallacy will now be retired—gracefully or otherwise—and give rise to a renewed determination to understand and overcome the problems of institutional care for our elders.

REFERENCES

1. Riley, M. W., and Foner, A., *Aging and society. V. 1: An inventory of research findings*, N.Y., Russell Sage Foundation, 1968.
2. Markson, E. W., and Hand, J., Referral for death: Low status of the aged and referral for psychiatric hospitalization, *Aging and human development*, 1970, *1*, 261-272.
3. Kastenbaum, R., and Aisenberg, R. B., *The psychology of death*, N.Y., Springer, 1972.

*A notable exception is the recent inquiry into "Death with Dignity" conducted by the U.S. Senate Special Committee on Aging, chaired by Sen. Frank Church (August 7-9, 1972).

part one

MAINTENANCE IN THE COMMUNITY

chapter 2

LIVING CONDITIONS AND EVERYDAY NEEDS OF THE ELDERLY WITH PARTICULAR REFERENCE TO SOCIAL ISOLATION[1]

Ruth Bennett, Ph.D.

One of the major distinguishing social characteristics of the aged is their isolation. Social isolation, or perhaps social marginality, is the absence of meaningful social roles or rolelessness. The very names by which the social positions of the aged are designated imply that former role partners are not available for support, nurturance, stimulation, interest-sharing, or other forms of social interaction. Terms like widow or widower and retiree or emeritus imply the absence of role partners. Social isolation may be thought of as socially induced sensory or stimulus deprivation.

Many factors beyond the control of any single aged person probably contribute to the social isolation of the aged. These are mandatory retirement policies and attendant meager financial resources, reduced mobility due to physical infirmity, deaths of spouse, relatives, friends and other age peers, social and geographic mobility of offspring and widespread prejudice against the aged.

[1] Revised version of invited lecture given at the 9th International Congress of Gerontology, Kiev, U.S.S.R., July 2–7, 1972.

NEGATIVE ATTITUDES OF THE SOCIALLY ISOLATED AGED

Isolation of the aged occurs against a background of pervasive negative stereotypes of the aged and negative attitudes toward aging. According to a recent review, these negative attitudes are found cross-nationally, among old and young people alike and among people who work with the aged, as well as those who do not. Ruth Bennett and Judith Eckman [1] noted that while there is not necessarily a cause and effect relationship between negative attitudes toward the aged and their social isolation, there seems reason to believe they are mutually reinforcing.

Little is known about absolute or relative numbers of social isolates among the aged cross-nationally, nor does it make sense to guess at them. Clearly the phenomenon of social isolation of the aged is well-known cross-nationally. Very recently, concern was expressed in a U.N. General Assembly report [2] on aging about the impact on the elderly of rapid urbanization and industrialization in newly developing countries, where young families are encouraged to move to cities, thereby abandoning the old in rural areas. Probably the rates of isolated, aged persons will increase, largely because most of the aged are women who are usually found in more marginal positions in society than men.

As has been noted many times but it bears repetition, the census report item of "living alone" probably is not a true indicator of social isolation in the aged. Unfortunately at this point in time there seems to be no agreement on an index of social isolation to be put into immediate use to survey the incidence of social isolation in the aged cross-nationally. However, there seems an urgent need to conduct such surveys.

Discussions containing varying degrees of both detail and empirical evidence about the concept of social isolation in the aged cross-nationally have appeared in many internationally known works [3-9]. Expression of concern about isolation of the aged in newly developed nations appeared in the United Nations General Assembly report previously cited.

Epidemiological surveys of the mental health of the community aged have been conducted in the United States and United Kingdom since the 1950s and some have collected some information on isolation. Some of the early U.K. surveys indicated that social isolation appeared to place the elderly at risk of developing mental illness or, at least, of hospitalization for mental illness. Kay, Beamish and Roth [10], found that in Newcastle-Upon-Tyne, 10.3% of those 65+ residing in the community were suffering from organic disorders as compared with 12.9% in mental hospitals, a difference of only 2.6%. The findings seemed to show that people with organic disorders can be maintained with equal facility out of institutions, but that those with functional disorders needed hospitalization, possibly due to their isolation. Indeed, 31% of those 65+ in the community were found suffering from functional disorders, while 42% in the hospitals were similarly impaired. This research team revisited Newcastle-Upon-Tyne several years later and found again that only a very small fraction of old people with psychiatric disorders were being cared for either as hospital inpatients or as residents of homes. Several small-scale U.S. surveys of the community aged conducted in the 1950s also indicated that there were many isolated, as well as mentally ill elderly persons at risk of hospitalization. Gruenberg [11] studied residents of Syracuse. This report may well have served as a background for the recent development of Gruenberg's [12] concept of social breakdown syndrome (SBS).

Perlin [13] studied elderly volunteers from the community near the U.S. National Institutes of Health. He found many to be impaired, but the extent to which they resembled inpatients was not studied. More recently the findings of Lowenthal and associates [14-16] suggest that while isolation is not directly related to mental disorder, presence of companions keeps the mentally ill aged out of hospitals.

Bourg [17] in a paper circulated by the Administration on Aging, questions the usefulness of the concept of rolelessness as it relates to aging. Basing some of his views on the research of Robert S. Weiss, Bourg writes that the "development of role theory and the application of a theoretical perspective on 'rolelessness' with regard to aging made much sense in the rapidly developing industrial society." Bourg [18] goes on to note that:

> today, further developments have brought changes not previously anticipated. . . . these directions point to the lessening significance of the stylized roles of an earlier, more steadily developing society.

He feels that a more,

> fruitful locus for empirical studies will be the basic assumptions and functions of various relationships, . . .
>
> We will draw near to the source and context of meaning for the participants in various situations whether indeed there may also be within their role alterations or increasing rolelessness.

Irrespective of whether we can answer the question of the future significance of rolelessness for the elderly, there appear to be many aged persons who are involuntarily isolated currently and who seem to be suffering from the consequences of such isolation.

For instance, there seems ample evidence indicating that there is a relationship between isolation and low morale, a concept sometimes used interchangeably with personal adjustment. Surveys have been conducted in a number of settings but have not yielded straightforward findings. As is indicated in the work of Britton [19] and Youmans [20] in rural areas, well-adjusted aged persons are found to be active, eager to participate, and able—well into old age. However, in large cities the variables of age density and adequacy of living conditions seem to intervene. Participation seems needed to preserve morale in the aged mainly where age density is low; that is, when there are not many other old people in a neighborhood according to Rosow [21]. In a housing project studied by Messer [22] presence of age-appropriate peer groups with age-appropriate normative expectations were thought to condition the correlation between isolation and low morale. In a recently completed, U.S. National Survey of 4,000 elderly persons, Schooler [23] found that the overall relationship between participation and morale was a weak one. The relationship seemed largely conditioned by whether or not old people perceived their surroundings as favorable. Schooler concluded that the morale of an elderly person may be low regardless of degree of isolation if he thinks of his poor housing conditions as a sign of rejection and neglect.

Our research, to which I will devote most of this paper has focused not only on the relationship between social isolation and variables such as social adjustment, mental status and cognitive functioning, but also on the development and evaluation of isolation-reducing programs. Our research on social isolation was begun 15 years ago with a study in which 100 case records of a home for aged were used to identify those characteristics which differentiated residents who were transferred to a mental hospital, from those who were not. Fifty residents of the home who were transferred were compared to controls matched for age, sex, and length of residence who remained in the home. The findings showed that poor scores on a combined index of social isolation experienced prior to entering the home were related to inability to get along with staff members and other residents, and sometimes resulted in transfer to a mental hospital. Based on this research, Tec and Granick [24] reported the following findings concerning the relation between pre-entry isolation and subsequent social adjustment:

1. Residents who were isolated prior to entry encountered significantly more difficulties in interacting with their peers ($X^2 = 14.6$, $p < .01$ and with rank order correlation, Tau was 1, $p < .01$)
2. Residents who were isolated prior to entry encountered significantly more difficulties in interacting with staff members ($X^2 = 8.3$, $p < .05$; Tau = 1)
3. Residents who were isolated prior to entry appeared to be more likely to be transferred out of the home to a mental hospital but this relationship was not significant.

Given the limitations of case record studies, a direct survey was undertaken by Granick [25] of 100 elderly residents, two-thirds of whom were women in their late 70s. One hundred consecutive admissions to the home were interviewed three times—once on admission, and again at one and two month intervals. Data on six month adjustment were collected from social work case records and from interviews with recreation workers in the home.

INDEX MEASURES DERIVED FROM THIS RESEARCH

The following measures were constructed from this research:

1. Adulthood Isolation Index (AII), which was a measure of the extent of lifetime role contacts with family friends, work and organizations.
2. Pre-entry Isolation Index (PII), which was a measure of number of social contacts outside the institution in the year prior to entry.
3. Socialization Index (SI), which was a measure of the amount of information learned about life in the home, consisting of questions about formal practices and informal norms in the home such as, "What kinds of activities are available during the day?"
4. Integration Index (II), which measured amount of participation in the home's activities.
5. Evaluation Index (EI), which measured how the resident felt about various aspects of life in the home such as the food and medical care.
6. Conformity Index (CI), which measured the extent to which the resident behaved in terms of the norms of the home.

In this research, social isolation experienced prior to entry as well as during adulthood was studied in relation to socialization, integration (participation), evaluation, and conformity. Social isolation was found to be inversely and significantly related to socialization and integration. There was no significant relation between isolation and evaluation (a concept similar to morale) or conformity after either one or two months of residence in the home. With time, however, there was an increase in the inverse relation between isolation and conformity. As length of residence in the home increased, isolated aged persons engaged in deviant behavior. One explanation for this delay, may be that it took time to learn to deviate or to learn the forms of deviance in the home.

The findings of Table 1 show that residents who experienced isolation before entering the home had difficulty becoming socialized. The relation between socialization and isolation was greater than the relation between isolation and any of the three components of adjustment. Desocialization or inaccurate perceptions of life in the home seemed to be an intervening factor mediating the relationship between isolation experienced prior to entry and subsequent poor adjustment.

In an article based on this work Granick and Nahemow [26] reported that scores on the PII ranged from 1-9 (0-10 was possible) with a median of 4.5. Over

Table 1. Rank-Order (Rho) Correlations Between Isolation, Socialization and Adjustment after One, Two and Six Months of Residence in a Home (N = 100)

Isolation and Socialization	*Socialization and Adjustment*								
	One Month				*Two Months*				*Six Months Adjustment*
	Socialization	Integration	Evaluation	Conformity	Socialization	Integration	Evaluation	Conformity	
Adulthood	.23[a]	.21[a]	.02	.00	.22[a]	.23[a]	.04	.11	.09
Pre-entry	.27[b]	.16	.07	.02	.27[b]	.22[a]	.08	.13	.19[a]
Socialization (1 Month)		.51[c]	.26[b]	.08	.79[c]	.50[c]	.12	.02	.32[c]
Socialization (2 Months)					–	.48[c]	.10	–.04	.26[b]

[a] $p < .05$
[b] $p < .01$
[c] $p < .001$

one-half of the respondents reported contact with fewer than five people in the year prior to admission and were regarded as isolated for that measure. Isolation related best to socialization and early or rapid socialization, rather than socialization *per se* related best to adjustment. That is, those with accurate perceptions of life in the home in the first month adjusted better than those who subsequently became socialized.

After two years, a follow-up study of the process of long-term social adjustment of residents of the home was undertaken by Bennett and Nahemow [27]. Changes in adjustment patterns over time, interrelations between components of adjustment, relations between early and late adjustment, and the relations between socialization and both early and later adjustment were studied. Forty-five residents who had been seen two years earlier were interviewed once more. Findings showed the relation between one month socialization and integration was stable over time. There was a systematic decrease in the correlation between socialization and evaluations with time, mainly because evaluations became differentiated. There was a continued increase in the relation of socialization to conformity, which had been indicated by the six-month social worker's adjustment report. The social worker's adjustment report was thought to reflect conformity more than any other behavior.

Patterns of Isolation

Four patterns of isolation were differentiated by Bennett and Nahemow [28]. They were:

a. Non-isolation
b. Old age non-isolation
c. Involuntary isolation
d. Voluntary isolation.

These patterns were studied in relation to socialization. Table 2 shows that all

Table 2. Relation Between Pattern of Isolation and Socialization at Two Months (N = 100)

Isolation Pattern	*Adulthood*	*Pre-entry*	*Socialization at Two Months: Number*	*Per cent Above Median*
Non-Isolate	Not isolated	Not isolated	31	77
Early isolate	Isolated	Not isolated	10	50
Involuntary isolate	Not isolated	Isolated	14	36
Voluntary isolate	Isolated	Isolated	45	29

patterns of isolation had negative effects on socialization, in contrast to non-isolation. The score differences between non-isolates and the group next in line were greater than between any two types of isolates. Pattern of isolation was obtained as follows:

1. Lifelong Isolates: those residents who had below median score on both the AII and the PII.
2. Old Age Isolates (Involuntary Isolates): those residents who had above median scores on the AII but below median scores on the PII.
3. Old Age Non-Isolates: Those residents who scored below the median on the AII but above the median on PII.
4. Lifelong Non-Isolates: those residents who scored above the median on both the AII and the PII.

While the lifelong (voluntary) isolates (who were, perhaps, mentally ill) did worst of all, it was not much worse than involuntary isolates. However, the gap widened between involuntary isolation and early isolation and widened most between early isolation and no isolation at all. The findings suggest there may be critical periods for isolation and that it may have more negative consequences for socialization if it occurs late in life and is uncompensated.

From the series of studies described above, it was concluded that the consequences of isolation are such that socialization and social adjustment to a home for aged are impaired. Age, sex, physical status, and other background factors did not relate systematically to isolation nor did they explain the obtained findings.

This led to the suspicion that there were two, or possibly more, "syndromes" which were related to similarly maladjusted behavior found among the elderly: one was mental disorder which probably resulted in hospitalization; the other has since been termed the 'isolation-desocialization' syndrome, for want of a better name. The 'isolation-desocialization' syndrome is a process that may follow this example: an old person in the community becomes isolated, then desocialized; he enters a home for the aged or some other setting, misperceives the norms and blunders socially soon after entry; others single him out, perhaps as a "troublemaker" and avoid him; he then becomes resentful and alienated; finally, he deviates further from the norms by becoming involved in overt conflict with staff members and/or other residents. Presumably, long experience with social isolation would not be as great a handicap to an old person who remained in the community as it is to one who is relocated and must adjust socially. However, also presumably, the effects of social isolation may be remediable, whereas those resulting from mental disorders of the senium are more nearly hopeless.

It was not clear from our early studies whether some of the maladjusted behavior observed was the result of the 'isolation-desocialization' syndrome, or of mental disorder; nor, did we know if both isolation and maladjusted behavior resulted from mental disorder. It was our good fortune to have working with us a visiting psychiatrist, trained in Britain, who wanted to study in a nonclinical manner the relationship between social isolation, mental disorder, and social adjustment in the aged. Fifty-three successive admissions who had been studied two years earlier were independently evaluated by the psychiatrist using a crude standard diagnostic form he designed to determine presence, or absence, of organic or functional mental disorder. This measure was designed to exclude data on early social isolation or social adjustment and was based largely on current cognitive functioning. Findings obtained by Walton, Bennett and Nahemow [28, 29] showed no relationship between social isolation and mental disorder.

Residents suffering from senile and/or arteriosclerotic dementia were differentiated from those with functional psychiatric disorders by their social adjustment patterns. Those with mild dementia adjusted to the institutional environment much like normal residents; those with functional disorders behaved much like social isolates. They were unhappy and did not live up to the expectations and requirements of other residents. Neither group of mentally disordered residents participated in the home's activities, in contrast to the normal residents.

The next series of studies which were conducted at the home were designed to determine if increased social interaction, in the form of actual admission to the home, improved social adjustment and cognitive functioning. Weinstock and Bennett [30], using whatever standard measures were available for cognitive performance and social adjustment and which could be administered to the aged both in and out of the home, studied waiting list persons, newcomers, and oldtimers. The relationships between isolation, socialization, mental state, and cognitive functioning–both on admission to, and after one year of residence at the home–were also studied.

The hour long, standard interview contained adaptations of all the measures used in earlier research described above and three additional measures–all of which were subtests of the Wechsler Adult Intelligence Scale (WAIS)–a standardized test of cognitive ability. The subtests used were:

1. Information, containing 20 questions measuring basic knowledge about topics ranging from names of composers to the colors of the American flag.
2. Comprehension, containing 14 items, designed to measure the ability to combine information into new forms.
3. Similarities, which included a measure of conceptualization with 13 items of paired association.

Test Scores

The distribution of means on the WAIS test scores for waiting list subjects, newcomers, and oldtimers are seen in Table 3. They show that on all the WAIS

Table 3. Mean Scores on Wechsler Adult Intelligence Scale (WAIS) Subtests and Socialization Index in Waiting List, Newcomer and Oldtimer Groups* (N = 100)

Mean WAIS Scores	*Waiting List Group*	*Newcomers*	*Oldtimers*
WAIS Information	13.10	15.00	13.55
WAIS Similarities	5.95	7.40	6.35
WAIS Comprehension	13.50	15.65	16.45
WAIS Total	**32.55**	**38.05**	**36.35**
Socialization Index	**10.10**	**18.50**	**20.30**

* Chi square were computed for differences found among groups for all tests. They were as follows:

WAIS information:	$Chi^2 = 2.73\ p < .10$
WAIS similarities:	$Chi^2 = 3.16\ p < .10$
WAIS comprehension:	$Chi^2 = 6.13\ p < .02$
Total WAIS:	$Chi^2 = 9.57\ p < .01$
Socialization Index:	$Chi^2 = 64.56\ p < .001$

subtests means were higher for the resident groups than for the waiting list group. The newcomers' scores on WAIS total and on all WAIS subtests with the exception of WAIS comprehension were higher than those of both the waiting list group and the oldtimers. Differences in mean total WAIS scores were significant at the .01 level across groups. Newcomers seemed to perform best, possibly because they were in the midst of being socialized. Oldtimers appeared to have reached a performance plateau. Waiting list persons performed worst of all; perhaps, because they were the most socially isolated in their own homes, and deprived of cognitive experiences and stimulation.

For newcomers, correlation coefficients for the relations between all WAIS subtests and the SI were significantly higher than for those of the other two groups. The correlation coefficients were as follows:

.77 for information and socialization,
.51 for similarities and socialization,
.78 for comprehension and socialization,
.74 for WAIS total and socialization.

Newcomers appeared to be highly involved in a salient learning experience which seemed to "spill over" to performance on tests of cognitive ability.

Age, *per se*, did not relate to poor cognitive functioning. The waiting list sample, although somewhat younger than the total resident sample, did not perform well on any tests. In general, when groups were divided at their median ages and younger residents were compared with older ones, the older ones performed better. This was specifically true of older residents in general but especially of older newcomers, who were found to have higher scores than the younger waiting list sample. This seemed to indicate that older residents benefitted most from increased stimulation in the home.

Similarly, education did not account for high scores. Since all groups had a similar high level of education, they should have performed alike at the outset. In point of fact, they did not. Level of education did not correlate with either WAIS subtests or the socialization measure. This was most evident in the newcomer group who, by virtue of being stimulated by involvement in the socialization process, were more likely to perform well on tests.

Residents as a group obtained markedly higher socialization scores than people on the waiting list, which came as no surprise since they knew more about life in the home. The waiting list group, despite some exposure to the admission interview and intake procedure, was largely unaware of norms and practices in the home. The mean SI score for the waiting list group was 10.1 out of a possible score of 30, which was the lowest score for the three groups. Oldtimers obtained higher socialization scores than newcomers; their mean was 20.3; the mean obtained by newcomers was 18.5. These differences were significant at the .001 level across the three groups. Unlike score patterns on the WAIS subtests, on which newcomers obtained the highest scores, socialization scores seemed to reflect increments in experience obtained with increased tenure in the home. The pattern of scores also indicated that the socialization measure and the WAIS measure, with the possible exception of WAIS comprehension, were independent of one another.

To determine if waiting list persons' scores actually increased after admission, a one year follow-up study was undertaken. Forty survivors of the waiting list, newcomer and oldtimer groups were seen again. As may be seen in Table 4, waiting list persons improved when they became newcomers, indicating a "spill-over" effect of socialization or, perhaps, increased motivation to perform

Table 4. Mean Scores on Wechsler Adult Intelligence Scale (WAIS) Subtests and Socialization Index for Interviews 1 and 2 for Survivors (N = 40)

	Waiting List		*Newcomers*		*Oldtimers*	
Subtest	*Time 1*	*Time 2*	*Time 1*	*Time 2*	*Time 1*	*Time 2*
WAIS Information	13.1	13.6	17.1	16.5	14.0	12.8
WAIS Similarities	6.6	8.8	8.6	9.4	6.9	4.8
WAIS Comprehension	13.9	14.9	17.1	16.5	17.0	14.1
WAIS Total	**33.7**	**36.6**	**42.8**	**42.5**	**37.9**	**31.6**
Socialization Index	**10.1**	**22.8**	**18.5**	**22.8**	**20.3**	**22.9**

on tests. Oldtimers and former newcomers, however, seemed to deteriorate. Perhaps, had the home continued to offer them salient learning experiences this would not have occurred. From these studies, it was concluded that isolation diminished cognitive and social performance while interaction stimulated good performance.

At one point in our series of studies, we looked for the brighter side of social isolation if there was one. We thought isolation may well have some salutary personality effects, possibly resulting in attitudinal independence, in the "rugged individualist" or "old codger" willing to do battle against any restraints. This was not found to be the case; in fact the opposite was true, as may be seen in the research of Nahemow and Bennett [31, 32].

In order to study the relation between isolation and attitudinal independence, ninety-six residents, all those who had been in the home for about two years, were interviewed twice by the two investigators. Persuasibility, the opposite of independence, was defined as the tendency to agree with contradictory opinions expressed by the two investigators. Social integration was measured sociometrically by using residents' friendship choices. One salient and one topic free measure of persuasibility were used. Paradoxically and unexpectedly, the socially isolated residents were attitudinally dependent, but socially deviant.

Therefore, the relationship between conformity to social norms, persuasibility and counternormative persuasion was also studied by Nahemow and Bennett [33]. While some residents were highly persuasible, no relationship was found between the persuasibility tendency and conformity to real social norms operant in the home. Highly conforming residents were found to be well-adjusted and most resistant to counternormative persuasive appeals. Conforming residents had positive evaluations of the home and regarded it as a positive reference group while simultaneously indicating a lack of interest in people and events outside the home. From this series of studies, it was concluded that conformity was less dependent on a general compliance tendency in one's personality than upon commitment to the norms and activities of the home.

A point made in a recent paper by Bennett and Sanchez [34] notes that there seems a need to distinguish the conformity which stems from commitment to and involvement in a group and the seeming conformity or persuasibility which stems from an intense need or desire found among isolates to be accepted into a group.

Results

From our research, as well as that of others, we concluded tentatively that the involuntary nature of social isolation and its attendant negative consequences indicate a great need for social policies, practices, and programs to combat isolation. It seems hardly necessary to repeat this idea, yet its repetition has not seemed to provoke any major programmatic efforts in this direction. This may be because the problem of social isolation of the aged seems insurmountable or because some of the solutions seem so simple, though expensive, that they have no news value.

Mensh [35] and Bennett [36] reviewed the various mental health and quasi-mental health programs developed in the U.S. to serve elderly community residents. According to Mensh, there is "significantly less than optimal availability of community care for older patients." In the U.S., special community psychiatry programs are not aimed specifically at the aged. In general such programs have vague aims, are not standard in their structure, compete among themselves and with other agencies, and contribute to a general atmosphere of fragmentation of service, which tends to confuse the aged. In an updated review of community mental health care for the aged in the U.S., Mensh [37] included as mental health programs any sort of program specifically aimed at the aged. He found there were no special psychogeriatric facilities for the aged, but included as community mental health programs for the aged the following:

a. Nursing homes, homes for the aged, V.A. domiciliaries (all of which serve less than 5% of those 65+).
b. Senior centers which serve only about one-third of those eligible to belong, and which offer no medical, psychiatric, or work services but which do provide information, referrals, food, and recreation.
c. Special programs such as the Foster Grandparent Program, which provide no health or psychiatric services.
d. Friendly Visiting Programs, which provide no health or psychiatric services.
e. Community mental health programs designed to serve people of all ages in which the aged are notably underrepresented.

In a U.S. nationwide survey of patterns of utilization of psychiatric services for the aged using NIMH statistics collected up to June, 1964, Rosen, et. al. [38] reported that persons 65 and over occupied about 30% of all public mental hospital beds and showed higher resident patient rates than any other age group. They then turned to the new approaches for reducing mental hospital resident populations, stressing community-based psychiatric and auxiliary services for the aged. They found only 8% of the aged were served on an outpatient basis. Only 2% of the aged were served in clinics, a figure which had not changed in the past decade. While an estimated 200,000 nursing home patients have mental disorders, their care was largely custodial. Of 175 mental health day care facilities available in 1965, only one was designed specifically for the aged. While 175 day care facilities accepted older patients, only about 200 persons aged 65 and over were served. Only 9% (19,000) private physicians' patients were 65 and over. Married people, in contrast to the widowed, were less likely to be institutionalized. There were marked differences in the care of the "young old" and the "old old." The "young old" (65-74) were treated; the "old old" (75+) received custodial care. Similar findings were reported by Kramer, et. al. [39] using more recent figures collected by the National Institute of Health.

Another reason for neglecting the problems of the isolated aged may be that those community programs which have been aimed specifically at the aged have not been evaluated systematically. Perhaps, it simply has been assumed they have not reduced isolation, or improved mental state, morale, social adjustment, cognitive functioning or any other process indicative of maladaptation in the aged. On the positive side, there are a few programs which seem to provide some mental health care to the aged in the community and which have been evaluated systematically. The findings on a treatment service in research conducted by Mitchell and Goldfarb [40] for the Visiting Nurse Service in New York City indicate that three-fourths of the community elderly were chronically but not mentally ill, and that a majority of them did not need hospital care. Seventy-four per cent of the old people at home were not thought by visiting nurses to need institutionalization, though 42% were reported as depressed. In 13% of the cases, the home situation was not deemed adequate and old age home or nursing home care was thought to be needed. Three per cent of the patients were sick enough to need referral to a general hospital. These proportions were found to resemble health estimates made by others of aged community residents. Silverman [41] described a program of services to the widowed and outlined first steps in a program of intervention for the fairly young elderly. Stotsky [42] randomly assigned comparable mentally ill, aged patients in state hospitals in Boston to remain in the hospital or to go to nursing homes. No changes in the course of mental or physical illnesses were found; however, death and rehospitalization occurred less in the nursing homes.

In England, several general approaches were taken simultaneously, but few programs have been evaluated to determine their impact on the isolation or mental or physical health of the aged. The several approaches taken simultaneously include establishing 1) geriatric facilities in mental hospitals, 2) clinic facilities based in general hospitals, and 3) psychogeriatric hostels geared to limited periods of institutionalization. They are described in papers by Grant [43], Whitehead [44, 45], Whitehead and Graham [46], Hoenig and Hamilton [47], Barton and Whitehead [48], Morton and Barker [49], Jones [50], and O'Brien, et al. [51].

One such English program was evaluated systematically by Sainsbury [52]. Findings showed that mentally-ill old people living at home did not get better or worse than those in hospitals; they also were not burdens to their families as had been feared.

As a result of the continued pervasive neglect of the needs of the isolated aged we were led to develop several experimental resocialization programs aimed at the isolated aged in the community and to develop assessment techniques so that their impact could be evaluated systematically.

THE TEACHERS COLLEGE FRIENDLY VISITING PROGRAM

Only one of these experimental programs will be described. It is the Teachers College Friendly Visiting Program (TC-FVP) which we have been conducting for the past four years. The TC-FVP was developed by several groups of graduate students and some faculty members in an Administration on Aging (AoA) supported training program in gerontology. They sought out isolated aged persons in the Morningside Heights health catchment area, a high crime rate, densely populated, apartment dwelling section of New York City surrounding Columbia University, to whom they administered questions imbedded in a standard visit format.

It was recognized by all who participated that there are several Friendly Visitor Programs in operation in the U.S. Among other such programs there are the a) Family and Children's Service, Inc. of Monmouth County, New Jersey; b) Project FIND in New York City described in NCOA [53]; c) Project PATH in New York City; d) Project PILOT in New York City; e) Friendly Visiting Project of the International Ladies' Garment Workers Union's (ILGWU) [54], and f) the San Francisco Program for the "Hard to Reach" Older Persons, described by Estelle Booth [55].

However, none of these programs had been evaluated systematically to determine if they reduced isolation and/or some of its presumed effects.

Pilot research for the TC-FVP was conducted during the first two years to determine if it was possible to locate isolated elderly persons, if they would cooperate in a study, and if measures could be developed to assess as unobtrusively as possible the behavior of old persons residing in their own homes.

The FVP was expected to reduce social isolation by reconnecting the elderly to others, by indicating an awareness of their presence in the community, and by showing concern with their well-being. Initially, improved morale as well as improved social and personal adjustments and mental states were also expected to result from this program. The friendly visitors were thought to not only help reduce isolation but also attendant feelings of abandonment, as well as feelings of loneliness, depression, and anxiety. Moreover, by providing opportunities to engage in discussion they were expected to bring about improvement in some cognitive aspects of the mental state of the elderly persons visited. The pilot work to develop extensive interview and observation schedules was conducted over a two year period by Ruth Bennett, et al. [56, 57].

In the most recent and methodologically sound study in this series, conducted by Sr. Mary Anne Mulligan [58] for her Ed.D. thesis eight graduate students were paired in order to visit and assess twelve isolated aged community

Table 5. A Comparison of Selected Scores of Persons In and Not In the Teachers College Friendly Visiting Program (TC-FVP)

Persons in the Friendly Visiting Program (Experimental Group)	*Persons not in the Friendly Visiting Program (Control Group)*
Age: 76	79
Past Month Isolation Score:	
1st Visit (N = 12)	1st Visit (N = 13)
$\overline{X}$ = 1.3	$\overline{X}$ = 2.4
12th Visit (N = 12)	12th Visit (N = 12)
$\overline{X}$ = 1.3	$\overline{X}$ = 2.3
Grooming (Rating of Neat and Clean):	
1st Visit = 92%	54%
Visit = 92%	54%
Apartment (Rating of Neat and Clean):	
1st Visit = 63%	54%
12th Visit = 82%	54%
Number of Ailments Reported:	
1st Visit = 1.9	2.7
12th Visit = 1.9	3.1

residents who comprised the experimental group. The experimental group was visited every two weeks for a total series of twelve visits and were assessed at each visit. Another pair of graduate students assessed twelve persons matched approximately for age and also for sex and whether or not they were isolated; they formed the control group. The control group was visited to collect data only twice; these data were comparable to those collected at the initial and final visits with the experimental group. Some findings based on early data analyses are shown in Table 5.

The data in Table 5 indicate that Past Month Isolation scores were not affected by the friendly visitors. That is, those visited frequently did not rush out and become more social as a result of the visits; nor did the old people in the control group do so. Both the experimental and control groups remained socially isolated over time. However, it should be remembered that the experimental group received visitors from the TC-FVP program and, therefore, was considered to be less isolated for the duration of the experiment.

Personal grooming was initially better in the experimental group than in the control group; however, both groups remained constant in their personal grooming ratings. On the other hand, apartment upkeep improved in the experimental group only. Neither group initially complained of many physical ailments. The number of complaints however, about ailments, went up only in the control group.

Unfortunately, detailed visiting progress or case reports, many of which are of great interest, cannot be presented here. However, one case described in detail by Audrey Harris [59] will be briefly summarized to illustrate the extent of neglect experienced by an isolated aged person residing in the community:

> Mrs. D., age 83, received three negative ratings on a 12 item physical health observation schedule. She had swollen legs, swollen ankles, and a bandaged wrist. She claimed she only visited a "foot doctor" and never saw a medical doctor. She took many pills. Her vials of medications were unclearly marked for Rx, dates, and dosages. Of the assortment of some 12 vials, only two were labeled–but their dates were smeared. She lacked knowledge of what the pills were. On the only two of the 12 labels which were legible, the names Digoxin and Hydrodiuril were found both of which require a degree of intact intellect for proper dosage and usage.

Other, similar case reports have caused those in the TC-FVP to make a concerted effort to link our program with community hospitals and agencies willing and able to provide medical as well as multiple services to the elderly residing in the community. (Thus far, we have received no funds to support this program, though several agencies seem interested in it.) Six month follow-up visits to all, found most of the experimental group home, and most of the control group in institutions.

It is too soon to draw any definitive conclusions about the impact of the TC-FVP in particular, and friendly visiting programs in general. However, the presence of visitors does seem to have some direct, salutary effects particularly on behavior which can be influenced by frequent visiting, namely grooming of one's surroundings and amount of complaining about illnesses.

It is necessary but difficult to summarize all of our research on social isolation, its consequences, and the programs which may possibly combat it. We, as well as others, have located extremely isolated aged persons who reside in the community. We are convinced by them as well as by results of all of our early correlational studies that social isolation has a negative impact on the aged: it desocializes them, hampers social adjustment, and seems to reduce independence. At the present time, isolation in the aged does not seem to be correlated with the usual demographic factors, though my suspicion is that women are more readily rejected than men when they age. Isolation is not synonymous with mental disorder though it may result in some behavior patterns associated with mental disorder–specifically poor social adjustment, and poor cognitive functioning. If not compensated for in time, the effects of isolation may lead to serious and, possibly, irreversible impairments–cognitive and other. However, unlike senile mental disorders, the effects of isolation may be reversible through resocialization programs, such as those consisting of friendly visiting, which we have been developing and systematically evaluating.

Until rejection and other social stresses concomitant with aging are out of the picture, many of the aged probably will be at risk of developing physical, behavioral, and emotional disabilities which may have little if anything to do with the aging process *per se*–and much to do with isolation and neglect.

REFERENCES

1. Bennett, R. and Eckman, J., Attitudes in the U.S. aged: a critical survey of the literature 1950-70 aimed at determining gaps in knowledge. Paper read at meeting of American Psychological Association's Task Force for the White House Conference on Aging. Washington, D.C., June 20-22, 1971. (Proceedings in press.)
2. U. N. General Assembly, Question of the Elderly and the Aged. Note by the Secretary General to the 26th session; Item 55 of the provisional agenda, 1971.
3. Pagani, A. *Social isolation in destitution*. Milano, N. D., ca. 1956.
4. Kutner, B., Fanshel, D., Togo, A. M. and Langner, T. S. *Five hundred over sixty: a community survey of aging*. New York: Russell Sage, 1956.
5. Barron, M. L. *The aging American*. New York: Thomas Y. Crowell, 1961.
6. Cumming, M. E. and Henry, W. E., *Growing Old*. New York: Basic Books, 1961.
7. Tunstall, J. *Old and Alone*. London: Routledge and Kegan Paul, Ltd., 1966.
8. Shanas, E., Townsend, P., Wedderburn, D., Friis, H., Milhøj, P. and Stehovwer, J. *Old People in Three Industrial Societies*. New York: Atherton Press, 1968.
9. de Beauvoir, S., *La Viellesse*, Paris: Gallimard, 1970. Translated by Patrick O'Brian into English as *The Coming of Age*, New York: Putnam, 1972.
10. Kay, D. W., Beamish, P. and Roth, M. Old age and mental disorders in Newcastle-upon-Tyne I, *British Journal of Psychiatry*, 1964, 110 (465).
11. Gruenberg, E. M. *A mental health survey of older persons*. N. Y. State Department of Mental Hygiene Report, 1956.
12. Gruenberg, E. M., Snow, H. B., and Bennett, C. C. Preventing the social breakdown syndrome. *Social Psychiatry*, 1969, 47, 179-195.
13. Perlin, S. Psychiatric aspects of senile nervous diseases: Part I. A normal control study. Paper presented at 4th International Congress of Gerontology, Merano, 1957.
14. Lowenthal, M. F. Social isolation and mental illness in old age. *American Sociological Review*, 1964, 29, 54-70.
15. Lowenthal, M. F. Antecedents of isolation and mental illness in old age. *Archives of General Psychiatry*, 1965, 12, 245-254.
16. Lowenthal, M. F. and Berkman, P. L. *Aging and Mental Disorder in San Francisco*. San Francisco: Jossey Bass, 1967.
17. Bourg, C. J. Aging: role, rolelessness and relations. Theoretical background for research grant AA 4-69-101-01, "Lifestyles and mobility patterns of aging persons," circulated for administrative use by Administration on Aging, HEW, N.D., ca. 1971.
18. Bourg, C. J., page 14.
19. Britton, J. H. Change in adjustment of older community residents after six years. Paper presented at the 6th International Congress of Gerontology, Copenhagen, 1963.
20. Youmans, E. G. Orientations to old age. *The Gerontologist*. 1968, 8(3), 153-158.
21. Rosow, I. *Social integration of the aged*. New York: Free Press, 1967.
22. Messer, M. Possibility of an age-concentrated environment becoming a normative system. *The Gerontologist*, 1967, 17(4), 247-251.
23. Schooler, K. K., The relation between characteristics of residential environment, social behavior, and the emotional and physical health of the elderly in the United States. Paper presented at the 8th International Congress of Gerontology, Washington, D. C., 1969.
24. Tec, N. and Granick, R. Social isolation and difficulties in social interaction in residents of a home for aged. *Social Problems*. 1959, 7, 226-232.
25. Granick, R. Social isolation, socialization, and social adjustment in residents of a home for aged. Unpublished Ph.D. thesis, Columbia University, 1962.
26. Granick, R. and Nahemow, L. D., Preadmission isolation as a factor in adjustment to an

old age home. In P. Hoch, and J. Zubin, (Eds.) *Psychopathology of Aging.* New York: Grune and Stratton, 1961, pp. 285-392.

27. Bennett, R. and Nahemow, L., A two year follow-up study of the process of social adjustment in residents of a home for the aged. Paper read at annual meetings of the Gerontological Society, Los Angeles, 1965.
28. a) Bennett, R. and Nahemow, L. The relations between social isolation, socialization and adjustment in residents of a home for aged. In M. P. Lawton (Ed.), *Mental Impairment in the Aged.* Philadelphia: Maurice Jacob Press, 90-108, 1965.
    b) Walton, H., Bennett, R. and Nahemow, L. Psychiatric illness and adjustment in a home for aged. In J. Zubin, (Ed.), *Can Psychopathology be Measured*? Annals of the New York Academy of Sciences, 1964, 105, 897-918.
29. Walton, H., Bennett, R. and Nahemow, L. The significance of psychiatric symptomatology for social adaptation. *British Journal of Psychiatry.* 1964, 110, 544-548.
30. Weinstock, C. and Bennett, R. From "waiting on the list" to becoming a "newcomer" and an "oldtimer" in a home for the aged: two studies of socialization and its impact upon cognitive functioning. *Journal of Aging and Human Development.* 1971, 2(1), 46-58.
31. Nahemow, L. and Bennett, R. Persuasibility and persuasion in the aged. Paper presented at the meetings of the Eastern Psychological Association, Atlantic City, 1965.
32. Nahemow, L. and Bennett, R. Social adjustment and persuasibility in two branches of a home for the aged. Paper presented at the meetings of the American Psychological Association, Chicago, 1965.
33. Nahemow, L. and Bennett, R. Conformity, persuasibility and counternormative persuasion. *Sociometry.* 1967, 30(1), 14-25.
34. Bennett, R. and Sanchez, E. Psychopathology or deviance; treatment or intervention. In M. Hammer, K. Salzinger and S. Sutton, (Eds.), *Psychopathology.* New York: John Wiley & Sons, Inc., 1972, pp. 75-90.
35. Mensh, I. N. Studies of older psychiatric patients. *The Gerontologist*, 1963, 3(3), 100-104.
36. Bennett, R., Community mental health programs with specific reference to those for the aged. Paper read at Summer Institute of the Gerontological Society, Ashville, 1971.
37. Mensh, I. Community mental health and other health services for the aged. Paper presented at the meeting of the American Psychological Association's Task Force for the White House Conference on Aging, Washington, D. C., June 20-22, 1971. (Proceedings in press.)
38. Rosen, B. M., Anderson, T. E., and Bahn, A. K. Psychiatric services for the aged: a nationwide survey of patterns of utilization. *Journal of Chronic Diseases*, 1968, 21, 167-177.
39. Kramer, M. Taube, C. A. and Redick, R. W. Patterns of use of psychiatric facilities by the aged, past, present and future. Paper read at meeting of American Psychological Association's Task Force for the White House Conference on Aging. Washington, D. C., June 20-22, 1971. (Proceedings in press.)
40. Mitchell, D. L. and Goldfarb, A. I. Psychological needs of the aged patients at home. *American Journal of Public Health*, 1966, 56(10), 1716-1720.
41. Silverman, P. R. Services to the widowed: first steps in a program of preventive intervention. *Community Mental Health Journal*, Spring, 1967, 3(1), 37-44.
42. Stotsky, B. A systematic study of therapeutic interventions in nursing homes. *Genetic Psychology Monographs.* Nov., 1967, 76, 257-320.
43. Grant, J. Local health authority service for care of the aged. *Gerontologia Clinica.* 1967, 9, 230-235.
44. Whitehead, J. A. A comprehensive, psychogeriatric service. *The Lancet.* Sept. 18, 1965, 583-586.

45. Whitehead, J. A. Day care for elderly psychiatric patients. *British Journal of Geriatric Practices*. Sept., 1967, 4(3), 159-165.
46. Whitehead, J. A. and Graham, J. V. Boarding out elderly psychiatric patients, mimeo (N.D.)
47. Hoenig, T. and Hamilton, M. Extramural care of the elderly. *The British Journal of Psychiatry*, 1967, 113(497), 435-433.
48. Barton, R. and Whitehead, J. A., A psycho-geriatric domiciliary emergency service. *British Journal of Psychiatry*, January 1968, 114 (506), 107-108.
49. Morton, E. V. B. and Barker, M. E. 'The present nonsense' and the elderly sick. *The Practitioner*, June, 1968, Vol. 200, 819-823.
50. Jones, K. S. Further portrait of a psycho-geriatric hostel. *Gerontologia Clinica*, 1968, 10, 81-87.
51. O'Brien, T. D., Roberts, J., Brackenridge, G. R. and Lloyd, W. H. Some aspects of community care of the frail and elderly: the need for assessment, *Gerontologia Clinica*, 1968, 10, 215-227.
52. Sainsbury, P. Principles and methods in evaluating community psychiatric services. Paper presented at 8th International Congress of Gerontology, Washington, D. C., 1969.
53. National Council on Aging (NCOA). *The golden years: a tarnished myth*, Report prepared for O.E.O. by Jack Ossofsley, Project Director, Washington, D.C., 1970.
54. ILGWU Retiree Service Department, After a life of labor: a pioneering union's program for retirees, New York, 1971.
55. Booth, E. Involving the 'hard to teach' older persons in social activities. Paper read at the annual meeting of the Gerontological Society, Los Angeles, 1965.
56. Bennett, R., Sanchez, E., Block, H. Sr., Green, K. A., Sr., Halpin, M., Sr., Meade, M. R., Sr., Mulligan, M. A., Sr. and Neary, J. M., Sr. Development and evaluation of a friendly visitor program for the community aged. Paper read at the annual meeting of the Gerontological Society, Toronto, 1970.
57. Bennett, R. and Sanchez, E., New concepts in services to the aging: progress in the development and evaluation of a friendly visitor program for the community aged. Paper read at the annual meetings of the New York State Parks and Recreation Association, Monticello, 1971.
58. Mulligan, Sr. M. A., Further development and evaluation of a friendly visitor program for the isolated aged, Unpublished Ed.D. thesis, Teachers College, Columbia University. (In Preparation.)
59. Harris, A. Case reports on friendly visits. Submitted to R. Bennett, as a term paper. Teachers College, Columbia University, 1972.

chapter 3

A SUCCESSOR MODEL FOR COMMUNITY SUPPORT OF LOW-INCOME MINORITY GROUP AGED[1]

Sylvia K. Barg and Carl Hirsch

INTRODUCTION

In previous work the authors, in collaboration with others, have focused attention upon low-income minority group aged in the urban communities in which they reside (Kent, Barg, 1969). This focus has included an emphasis upon the role of indigenous community workers as liason agents between the members of the deprived minority and the social welfare system functioning to serve them. Positive results have been reported in training programs to heighten communication skills of indigenous workers, as well as to develop referral and advocacy skills among community workers with the aged (Kent, Hirsch, Barg, 1969, 1971; Kent, Hirsch, 1971).

In a further development Kent (1970) and Brody, Finkle, and Hirsch (1972) report on an experimental program designed to foster outreach by the Philadelphia County Board of Assistance to insure public supportive services to minority group aged in low-income areas of the city including populations of black ghetto areas. While the program focused on the referral and advocacy skills of community workers to insure the elderly residents' rights to minimal supports for community living, attention was also given to the development of "gatekeepers" in the community. The gatekeepers are persons who in resident or work roles in these communities are in touch with the elderly populations in their normal role activities and who, through program contact, are informed of the supportive services and procedures for obtaining social, health, and economic supports for

[1] An earlier version of this paper was presented at the Twenty-fourth Annual Meeting of the Gerontological Society, Houston, Texas. October 28, 1971.

the aged. Ideally, the result of concentrated program inputs would have resulted in both (1) the invigoration of the aged population through close contact with the skilled community workers who provide a role model for aged individuals and (2) the development of legitimate community advocates for the aged within the social structure of the low-income community. Unforeseen developments in program administration led to the abortion of advocacy procedures and inhibition of gatekeeper development as reported by Brody, Finkle, and Hirsch (1972).

However, some conceptual gaps in the structure of the experimental program did not become obvious until the process was underway. Failure to recognize the impact of long isolation for some aged and the decline in social integration through role loss for many others among the deprived minority groups comprising the target population placed unrealistic demands upon aged individuals. They were expected to move from states of fear and dependency (Kent, Hirsch, 1971; Kent, 1970) to confident self-representation with respect to the service bureaucracies existing and functioning in their communities. The goal of institutional change in these areas was to have been accomplished with support for the aged that was too meager considering the nature of both the aged groups' status in the community and the resistance to change by service institutions and government itself. While the support and positive role model provided by the community workers and the potential role of the gatekeeper could have led to improved conditions among the aged in low-income communities, the outcome still conceptualized a state of dependency by the aged on community agents vigorously acting in advocacy roles. Overlooked was (1) the need for structured roles for the aged fostering interaction among peers in their community and (2) the role of interaction as a theoretical prerequisite for both personal integrity or personality coherence and social activity, including self-representation in the community.

While building upon previous positive experience with community workers in work with the aged, Model Cities Senior Wheels East incorporates both case and group work techniques in urban neighborhood applications to form a model for an approach to meet the critical needs of individual aged. At the same time, it provides the basic means for alleviating the social conditions contributing to the reoccurrence of individual problems, i.e., self-representation of the aged themselves through group participation and group advocacy to gain service rights.

INTERACTION THEORY: THEORETICAL UNDERPINNINGS OF THE MODEL CITIES SENIOR WHEELS EAST APPROACH[2]

Arnold Rose (1964) refers to the implicit acceptance of symbolic interactionist theory in social gerontology from inception of the field in the work of Ernest Burgess and others. However, this orientation became formalized only as late as 1961 and 1962 when disengagement theory had already been introduced. To both Rose (1961) and Cavan

[2] In adopting the program, the Model Cities Administration in Philadelphia placed operational responsibility with two delegate agencies. The Model Cities Senior Wheels West Program is operated by the Wharton Centre, a long-established multiprogram agency. Model Cities Senior Wheels East is operated by the Olde Kensington Redevelopment Corporation, a recently established nonprofit organization of community residents working for the physical rehabilitation of housing and social change. While sharing program goals the two delegate agencies follow somewhat different approaches in their work in their respective communities.

(1962), adjustment of the individual to himself in his own old age is interdependent with adjustment to the persons and groups in his social world. Both authors agree on the importance of retirement or loss of occupation, decline in physical powers, and a new adjustment to the family and/or other primary groups, such as peer and friendship groups, as crucial to understanding and appreciating the situation of the aged. Reevaluation by the aged of themselves in the context of changed roles results. The difficulty of this adjustment is increased when we appreciate that the aged person is moving from a set of structured roles, positively evaluated within the society, to a set of ill-defined roles that receive less powerful positive evaluation, if not distinctly negative evaluation, in the social world. To Kent, the aged are "structured out" (1968).

Both Rose and Cavan would agree with Clark (1967) in her reference to Benedict's finding that "... cultural discontinuities ... always involve strain for the individual; however, when persons confronted with such discontinuities are fortified by 'a solid phalanx' of social grouping, they can often swing between remarkable extremes of opposite behavior without apparent psychic threat" (Clark, 1967, p. 442). This assertion is supported by data from Clark's San Francisco study as is its alternative: "... where the aging individual is released from earlier adult roles without either real or symbolic inter-relationships upon which to build self-esteem he often suffers a serious, stress-ridden discontinuity" (Clark, 1967, p. 442).

The situation of the aged person is then seen to be dependent on the interrelationship of his ties to formally organized and positively evaluated structures and of the degree of firm supportive ties he experiences in the more informally structured groups of which he is part. Cavan discusses the inability of recreation clubs to substitute for lost occupation or child-care activity in provision of equivalent roles since the positive self-conceptions developed through interaction or participation in these latter groups "... are often limited ... in that they may not be capable of expression in any group except the club itself" (Cavan, 1962).

Rose sees a more effective alternative for the development of equivalent roles in the process of development of a subculture of aging. The process of development of the subculture described by Rose can be seen to represent an interactionist perspective. Rose identifies the interaction of aged with one another on the bases of affinity, as a key factor in the potential development of a subculture. Second, the exclusion of the aged from interaction across age-grades reinforces the affinity within the old age group (Rose, 1962, p. 29). With the development of positive subcultural evaluations of new roles substituting for the neutral or negative evaluation of such roles in the wider culture, the aged person is helped to reestablish a positive self-concept in a changed context. While the approach to be described here recognizes the validity of the tenets of interaction theory as providing a viable perspective within which work with minority group aged residents of low-income neighborhoods can be carried out, there are further considerations of the special status of minority group aged that make the conceptions of individual-group adjustment presented in interaction theory even more compelling.

LOW-INCOME MINORITY GROUP AGED AS AN OPPRESSED MINORITY: POLITICAL CONSIDERATIONS IN THE MODEL CITIES SENIOR WHEELS EAST APPROACH

The problems which have occurred in the lives of those aged people identified and served in the first year of the program and the emergence of new problems among them following first contact are not seen as random events which will be unlikely to reoccur. They are seen as typical events in the lives of the aged poor and especially of those who are members of racial and ethnic minority groups as well. The assertion of the normality of reoccurring crises in the lives of the target population of the program is based on a view which decidedly does *not* see the cause of these problems resulting from failures of the older people themselves. The assertion stems from a view of the aged as members of a minority group which is discriminated against and systematically cut off from access to the resources of society which allow younger residents of these same areas a somewhat greater degree of independent functioning and greater control over their circumstances. The degree to which both younger and older members of this community are members of racial or ethnic minorities complicates the difficulties experienced by all age groups in their efforts to control their own lives and the conditions which serve as parameters of their social existence.

We then see the problems existing in the lives of the target population of this program resulting from the identification of the *individual* aged as members of a *disadvantaged group.* They are disadvantaged especially in terms of role loss and reduced economic means as discussed above. However, disadvantage also stems from the passivity of these persons. Passivity may have been present in previous life activity, but it becomes especially reinforced when "old age," as society defines it, is reached; social and economic incapacities are increased while physical health resources tend to decrease. Passivity extends throughout the life of the aged as citizens. It is unreasonable to expect that the low-income minority group aged can successfully serve in their citizen roles since political participation generally means group participation and the aged increasingly lose group identification and opportunities for interaction. This passivity is especially limiting since what is required to resolve the problems of the aged is a basic shift in values and national priorities so that the aged do not continue to be consigned to a second-class citizenship. They must be as highly valued as a group as any other within the society if the disadvantages they now suffer are to be removed. This is generally recognized as an outcome achievable only through political self-representation and consequent political power.

In this view we have a situation in which the aged—as members of a minority group per se,—lack resources to cope with changes in their social, economic, and physical health conditions. Their situation is then compounded by their placement in a community that has been characterized by low-income minority populations for many years. Concomitant with this is an absence of adequate social, economic, and health resources to meet the needs of the population and an absence of political power to gain the necessary resources.

We must anticipate the development of crises or problems in the lives of these older people under these conditions. Although many problems existing during the first year of the program of individual aged persons were dealt with, we recognize that these problems are only symptoms of the underlying individual and community disability reinforced throughout the years. Continued treatment of the problems alone is one alternative for program activity which would guarantee a busy workload for the staff. Service, however, would remain at a treatment level where only the symptoms and not the underlying conditions were dealt with. The program can attempt to confront and attempt to overcome the underlying conditions, at the same time that the painful social symptoms experienced by the older persons are treated, through the combination of case and group work techniques applied in the neighborhoods of residence of the deprived minority groups.

THE MODEL CITIES SENIOR WHEELS EAST PROGRAM

Conclusions concerning the role of interaction and group involvement in adjustment and functional ability levels achieved and maintained by the aged, together with social-political analysis of the present situation of low-income minority group aged provide the conceptual bases for this outreach program which deals with critical personal problems of aged in the target area and attempts, through community organization and group work techniques, to eliminate the personal vulnerability of individual members of the aged group.

In the first year of program activity, community workers canvassed the total target area on a door-to-door basis from the mobile office unit and uncovered numerous cases of aged persons with critical problems. Community workers participated with the aged in referral and advocacy capacities and placed pressure upon service institutions to respond to client needs. As well as having contributed to worker acceptance in the neighborhoods of the target area, this technique served to move many aged from a level of mere subsistence to more firm existence within the community as incomes increased, housing conditions improved, health problems received regular treatment, and personal or family problems were confronted. Where institutionalization was the only solution to the plight of some individual aged, the transition out of the community was facilitated.

While 7,620 contacts with households were attempted or completed, only 460 aged persons were served during the first nine months of activity. Fifty-two agencies were utilized and a total of 1,591 follow-up contacts were made to achieve satisfactory resolution to case problems.

Two citations from casework files illustrate two different outcomes relevant to the basic goals ofthe approach used. The first illustrates the movement of an aged woman to increased activism at the community level.

Mrs. A is seventy-three years old and has been elected to several community board positions with various community-based organizations. Her activity had been limited to attending meetings when it was convenient. She first came in contact with M. C. Senior Wheels East when she was invited to attend an Elders' Council meeting. Gradually she became more interested in the discussions of problems of senior citizens and then requested assistance to obtain Food Stamps. Although she had been receiving Social Security and Public Welfare Supplement (total = $138/month), she was not aware of the benefits of the Federal Food Stamp Program. Mrs. A knows nearly every senior citizen living within a three block radius of her home, and soon began referring others to our program for assistance.

Over the past months of association with Senior Wheels East, Mrs. A's community involvement has escalated. She participates fully in discussions of community problems, she has taken petitions and flyers to neighbors to alert them to certain actions or recommendations, she has been a key person in the formation of a new Senior Citizens group which has sponsored fund-raising events, and she attends other meetings of senior citizens as an information resource for them. She is taking a leadership role which she had not previously assumed—and is assuming corresponding responsibilities for action. She is now a regular member of the Elders' Council and recently was one of three who represented the council at a meeting with the governor of Pennsylvania to report the recommendations and demands of senior citizens.

The second case illustrates the success of the program in enabling continued community residence of an aged man who otherwise might have been institutionalized in his later years.

Mr. B expressed desire for employment and social activity to the Senior Wheels East worker during a regular door-to-door outreach effort of the program. Recognizing that Mr. B was depressed by his feelings of uselessness and isolation, the worker made arrangements for him to be employed as a maintenance man in the Senior Wheels East office. By having been offered this employment opportunity, he again felt useful and productive. Surrounded by people who cared about him, he was able to respond by caring about someone other than himself. His four weeks of employment also gave him the opportunity to evaluate his dreams and desires within the perspective of additional limitations which had come with age.

Although his missing finger on one hand had been his only physical limitation during his employment years, he now found that his general health could not withstand the demands of a regular part-time job. He did, nonetheless, begin attending and participating in every senior citizen meeting held in his neighborhood and derived tremendous joy just from anticipating the mailman's delivery of another meeting invitation. Several months after he made the decision that he was not well enough to work, following weeks in the hospital, he began to talk more openly about his living conditions and alternatives to working as means by which he could feel like somebody.

He had developed a good working relationship with his D.P.A. caseworker, as well as the hospital social worker. We held an interagency conference to discuss alternatives which Mr. B might consider. Shortly thereafter, he decided that foster home care placement under D.P.W. would be his first choice. This program places elderly in home/family settings where the elderly person is treated as "one of the family." Since the placement he has gained weight, is healthier, and is thoroughly pleased with his new family. Although it was necessary for Mr. B to make a transition from a familiar neighborhood, he was given every support to remain in a community setting. Through frequent case contact he became known as an individual with strengths and limitations, and his strengths were reinforced through the case contact as well as through the group contacts, even after employment. He was given supports which enabled him to select an alternative at a time when he was still able to do so, and thereby prevent the very imminent reality of institutionalization if a transition to more protected living was not made.

Although a major portion of community worker time in the first year was spent on outreach, referral, and advocacy on individual case problems, the community organization specialist on staff devoted full time to the organization of several neighborhood groups, establishment of liason and staffing relationships with some groups already existing, as well as organization of thirteen neighborhood meetings preparatory to an area-wide forum focusing on development of recommendations for the White House Conference.

Movement of individuals from client caseloads to social activity in the group structures was encouraged on the initial visit with clients, as well as on one-week, one-month, three-month, and six-month follow-ups with individual clients. Similarly, aged persons participating in group activity often moved to the client caseload after establishing rapport with the group worker and raising individual problems that required worker assistance for resolution. In the first nine months of program activity, 41 group activities were conducted with a total attendance of 657. This figure represents repeated participation by a large proportion of group members.

Fostering group participation by the aged through program activity is primarily based on the recognition of both the group nature of human social life and the losses in this regard experienced by the aged. Forced movement to social participation, or to social action following initial group participation, is *not* a practice of the program. Recognizing the variation in personal adjustment to social deprivation which exists among any large group of aged community residents, the basic approach of the program is to provide social alternatives for the aged within their social life space as well as the provision of activity alternatives, which range from bingo to social action within the groups.

A secondary goal of group initiation in the communities in which the program is active is the development of skills to maintain dynamic interaction within the groups which can enable their continuation beyond the life of this program. Included in this latter category of skills is both leadership development and transfer of techniques to achieve financial independence by the groups through their own efforts. Intergroup contact has been established through the formation of an Elders' Council consisting of representatives of each of the eleven functioning groups. The Elders' Council meetings serve as a monthly forum for the exchange of group experiences as well as an active advisory board to the program.

An example of group movement towards self-direction and operation of activities may be seen in the residents' club at an apartment house for the elderly which includes a large portion of Ukrainian Americans, many of whom are fluent only in Ukrainian. From an initial meeting in January of 1971 this group moved to committee structure and responsibility for the conduct of monthly meetings four months later. While not directly involved in social action programs outside of the apartment dwelling, the group has identified certain resident needs within the facility and has acted to provide resources to meet those needs. Participation by residents of this facility in Elders' Council meetings, joint trips with members of other racial and ethnic groups, and attendance at area-wide conferences on the mutual problems of the aged and workshops to develop action agendas have served to introduce the potential for externally oriented social action among members of this and other groups. Joint concern for lack of public transportation adequate to the needs of the elderly among members of all groups illustrates one potential area for collective social action by aged community residents who recognize the limited role that can be played in this respect by the mobile unit, the "wheels," of the Model Cities Senior Wheels program.

In another instance a neighborhood group, brought together through the joint efforts of Model Cities Senior Wheels East staff and Model Cities Housing Information Center staff decided to emphasize both their concern for deteriorated housing in their immediate neighborhood and their identity as senior citizens in their group name. Continued staffing by both programs of the Philadelphia Model Cities Administration has contributed to increased skills in group self-representation on the housing issue as well as recognition of potential social rewards from expansion of group interest to recreational activities as well as to other social issues on which action is possible. The community leadership potential of the group has been secured by their persistence and success in eliminating some housing hazardous to the community. The reintegration of the aged as a group into community decision-making processes has been begun in this one neighborhood by the activities of these concerned seniors.

RELATED CONSIDERATIONS FROM PROGRAM EXPERIENCE

Three issues concerning the community-workers staff's activity with the aged in this multifocus program are of special interest to the authors and deserve greater attention than can be given in this brief report.

(1) Inability to hire part-time community workers together with the strenuous nature of job tasks made the employment of elderly community workers impossible, although the need for the creation of such employment opportunities among the aged was fully recognized. Field work experience in previous community work with the aged (Kent, Barg, 1969; Kent, Hirsch, 1971; Kent, 1970) demonstrated the burden placed upon older workers by daylong door-to-door activity. Although performance of individual elderly workers was adequate, the perceived unpredictability of work demands at the initiation of this program led to a decision to forestall employment of the elderly.

However, the predominantly young and younger middle-aged community worker staff have not reported incidents of resentment from the target-aged population on the basis of age disparities. Indeed, group experiences involving younger workers have been extremely rewarding and dynamic. The experience of the program suggests that the demonstrated concern of younger people with the social problems of the aged group contributes to an enthusiastic commitment to confronting these problems through organized social action by the aged to a degree that might not be achievable if the community staff were composed only of the elderly. The potential for cross-generational alliances perceived by the aged activists might allow for greater optimism among them and this, in turn, can be seen to be related to the degree of activity undertaken. Similar observations of the role of young staff in group therapy sessions with institutionalized aged in stimulating improvement in personal appearance and willingness to participate actively have been reported by Dr. Maurice E. Linden (1954), consultant to Model Cities Senior Wheels East. Psychiatric explanation of increased enthusiasm in the group therapy setting involves a revitalization of libidinal energy on the personality level.

(2) In other work, the authors (Kent, Hirsch, Barg, 1969, 1971) have recognized concern expressed in the literature for the integration of indigenous community workers in professionally staffed agency settings. The maintenance of the workers' community perspective on issues of social policy while developing increased skills for the achievement of social change is accepted as a necessary combination if the rigidity of the social welfare establishment is to be successfully challenged by the incorporation of community workers in structured roles within agencies and if profound social change is to occur. However, if the agency continues to view the client population as composed of essentially atomized, dependent individuals and the agency approach is founded in this conception, the ability of the community workers to remain in work roles and maintain the perspective of their community, founded in their experience within that community, is seen to be minimal. Agency acceptance of a view of the target population as a politically powerless group, oppressed in their group identity, and an agency commitment to contribute to the liberation of that population will, on the other hand, lead to a

resolution of the apparent conflict suggested above. The attempt to achieve self-representation through group organization of the aged in this instance is viewed as a technique which will, at the same time, provide community workers with feedback from the community that is at least equivalent to feedback received from professionally oriented personnel, and can serve to contribute to the maintenance of their community perspective.

(3) A third consideration based on program experience with three groups of elderly in the target area who differ in racial and ethnic identity leads to conclusions that the basic approach utilized is appropriate to all three groups. We accept that cultural differences among black, Puerto Rican, and foreign-born white aged lead to differences in some patterns of adjustment to aging. However, impressionistic evaluations support the view that the common experiences of economic deprivation, loss of social roles and group supports associated with sociological aging, and declines in physical health associated with physiological aging combine to obviate cultural differences which each group brings to the experiences of sociological and physiological aging. Research findings from a study of black and white aged residents of low-income neighborhoods in Philadelphia (Kent, Hirsch, 1971) do point to differences between the two groups in terms of supports available in later life which can, in turn, be seen to result from differential access in earlier life to employment–security when employment was achieved, economic rewards of employment, and other opportunities associated with economic status. The role of racism in limiting access in earlier life can not be disregarded when evaluating the effects of early life experience found in later life. However, other minority groups in the same society and with whom the Model Cities Senior Wheels East has worked have endured similar oppression on social, economic, cultural, and personality levels, and the Model Cities Senior Wheels East approach has been effective in work with each group.

While the observations included in this section of the presentation were introduced with a statement recognizing the limited time and space for full discussion, it must be further conceded that the issues raised also require further well-documented study.

SUMMARY AND CONCLUSIONS

The bases of this multifocus approach to community work with low-income minority group aged in urban neighborhoods has been presented in the discussion of social theory and political ideas concerning the location of the aged in contemporary American society. The program's success has been suggested in the impressionistic material presented. However, limitations of information-referral-advocacy work with the aged when adequate services to support the aged in the community are only available in restricted quantity must be confronted.

The group work-community organization component of the work already undertaken is directed at achievement of political power by the aged to secure the necessary supportive services on a permanent rather than demonstration basis in all neighborhoods of the urban community. However, the achievement of appropriate levels of human services requires the elevation of human priorities in governmental structures nationally and the positive evaluation of the aged as a social group in the ideological segment of the social structure of the society. Work among the aged can contribute to the change in priorities, values, and material inputs to this group in the community but the involvement of other age groups within the society in this struggle must be seen as another force necessary to the achievement of the goals represented in this one service program.

Efforts to achieve funding to increase levels of necessary service to be delivered by the program are underway–but efforts to achieve this goal in other urban neighborhoods and in other cities where the aged reside must also be undertaken.

REFERENCES

Brody, S. J., Finkle, H., Hirsch, C. Benefit alert: Outreach program for the aged. *Social Work* 1972, *17,* 1.

Cavan, R. S. Self & role in adjustment during old age. In Arnold Rose, *Human behavior and social processes: An interactionist approach* Boston: Houghton Mifflin Co., 1962.

Clark, M. The anthropology of aging: A new area for studies of culture and personality. In *Middle Age and Aging: A Reader in Social Psychology,* Bernice L. Neugarten (ed.) Chicago and London: The University of Chicago Press, 1968, pp. 433-443.

Kent, D. P. Aging within the American social structure, *Journal of Geriatric Psychiatry,* 1968, *II,* 1.

———. *Benefit Alert Final Report.* Sociology Dept., The Pennsylvania State University, Spring 1970. Case studies presented in this report reveal the hesitancy of clients to request greater supports for fear of losing present supports.

Kent, D. P., Barg, S. K. From "N" to ego, *Social Casework,* April 1969.

Kent, D. P., Hirsch, C. *Needs and Use of Services Among Negro and White Aged: Volume I Social and Economic Conditions of Negro and White Aged Residents of Urban Neighborhoods of Low Socioeconomic Status.* Sociology Dept., The Pennsylvania State University, July 1971. Appendix D has interviewers' comments on respondents fears of losing present supports through challenging the status-quo.

Kent, D. P., Hirsch, C., & Barg, S. K. An antagonistic model of the rôle and training of indigenous workers with low-income aged. Paper presented at the 8th International Congress of Gerontology, Washington, D.C., August 1969.

———. Indigenous workers as a crucial link in the total support system for low-income minority group aged; A report of an innovative field technique in survey research, *Aging and Human Development, II,* 3, 1971, *2,* 189-196.

Linden, Maurice E. The significance of dual leadership in gerontologic group psychotherapy: Studies in gerontologic human relationships. *The International Journal of Group Psychotherapy, IV,* 3, 1954, *4,* 262-273.

Rose, A. Mental health of normal older persons. *Geriatrics,* September 1961, 459-464.

———. The subculture of aging: A topic for sociological research. *The Gerontologist,* 2, 123-127.

———. A current theoretical issue in social gerontology. *The Gerontologist, 4* 1964, *4.*

part two

ETHNOGRAPHIC ACCOUNTS: ENHANCING THE QUALITY OF LIFE

chapter 4

PRE-INSTITUTIONALIZATION FACTORS AS PREDICTORS OF ADJUSTMENT TO A LONG-TERM CARE FACILITY[1]

Sylvia Sherwood and Joyce Glassman
Clarence Sherwood
John N. Morris

INTRODUCTION

As part of a larger, longitudinal study of applicants to the Hebrew Rehabilitation Center for Aged (HRCA),[2] an instrument was devised which predicted in a highly reliable manner the judgments of an interdisciplinary clinical team[3] concerning which applicants to a home for the aged were More Suitable and which were Less Suitable for admission to that institution. (The HRCA is a long-term care facility in Boston that combines residential and chronic hospital functions.) This instrument has been described elsewhere (Sherwood and Feldman, 1969, 1970). Using these individualized diagnostic evaluations of need for admission as the criterion, data concerning 48 pre-coded items from home interviews were subjected to discriminant function analysis—a statistical technique for assigning population members into (usually) two clearly different

[1] This study is supported by NCHSRD Research Grant HS00470.
[2] Supported by U.S. Public Health Service Grants—Demonstration Project CH 23-26 and NCHSRD Research Grant HS00470.
[3] The interdisciplinary team included a physiatrist, an internist, a psychiatrist, a social worker, and a public health nurse.

groups. Eighty-three cases were used in deriving the discriminant function necessary for predicting team judgments and forty additional cases were used in testing the instrument.

Findings from the original discriminant function suggested five major areas of influence on team judgments concerning need for admission:

1. need for life maintenance services offered by the facility;
2. lack of opportunities for peer group relationships;
3. morale;
4. independence;
5. style of life.

An amended discriminant function was computed on the factors which made up the five conceptual areas in an effort to test the hypothesis. The success rate of the new discriminant function for predicting team judgments was 81.2% for the original sample of 83 cases and 73.6% for a new cross-validation sample of 53 cases. The results indicated the usefulness of these concepts for predicting team judgments concerning need for admission.

PROCEDURES AND INSTRUMENTS

This present study began in a pursuit of an answer to the question of whether the individuals selected by the prediction instrument as More Suitable would adjust better *to* institutionalization than those judged Less Suitable. This emphasis on adjustment *to* institutionalization as distinct from adjustment *in* the institution is fundamental.

Most of the studies in the literature dealing with the adjustment of the elderly and institutionalization have dealt, knowingly or not, only with adjustment in the institution. Comparative studies, for example, of institutionalized and in-the-community samples of elderly persons have generally found the institutionalized groups manifest poorer adjustment, as measured in a variety of ways including morale, self-esteem, social interaction, competence, and social cognition. One explanation advanced to account for these findings is that institutionalization has negative effects on the adjustment of the elderly. Another at least equally plausible hypothesis which also accounts for the findings is *selection*: individuals with poorer adjustment, lower morale, etc., are more likely to be institutionalized. The issue, then, as has been repeatedly pointed out in the literature (Anderson, 1967; Lieberman, Prock, and Tobin, 1968) and which is logically obvious upon perusal, is not whether the institutionalized elderly manifest poorer adjustment, lower morale, etc., than the non-institutionalized, but whether the institutionalized elderly manifest poorer or better adjustment (morale, etc.) in the institution than they would at the same point in time were they not in the institution. More sophisticated studies have attempted to deal methodologically with this problem by matching non-institutionalized individuals (in some instances, members of the waiting list for the same institution) with institutionalized individuals on a variety of characteristics (Anderson, 1967; Lieberman, Prock, and Tobin, 1968). Although these studies represent a great advance over simple comparisons of institutionalized and non-institutionalized groups, they have at least two important defects: 1) they are cross-sectional studies and thus cannot provide direct observations of changes in the adjustment, morale, etc., of elderly individuals—"change" in the institutionalized group can only be inferred on the basis of comparison with the non-institutionalized group and the validity of the inference is totally dependent upon the pre-institutional comparability of the two groups; 2) even where waiting list members have been used to construct the non-institutionalized matched sample, there is no assurance that all such individuals eventually become institutionalized—to the extent that they are withdrawn from the waiting list or die prior to institutionalization, they constitute a difference between the comparison groups, since by definition all of the institutionalized group were institutionalized.

The study being reported here has attempted to deal with the above-mentioned methodological difficulties 1) by obtaining adjustment measures at two points in time for a sample of applicants to HRCA; one segment of the sample, henceforth called the "Institutionalized Sample," was pre-tested in the community and post-tested after entry into HRCA; the other segment, henceforth called the "Waiting List Sample," was pre-tested in the community and post-tested while still on the waiting list for HRCA, and 2) by including in the waiting list sample only those persons who eventually (that is, subsequent to their post-test) actually entered the institution.

The sample for this study consists of 137 applicants to the Hebrew Rehabilitation Center for Aged, selected from a larger sample of 344 applicants to the Center (part of the earlier longitudinal study of applicants to the HRCA mentioned above). The 137 elderly persons constitute all who ultimately entered the Center and for whom pre- and post-measures were obtained.

The independent variable in the present study is the prediction of the team judgment concerning whether a person is More Suitable or Less Suitable for admission to HRCA as determined by the discriminant function instrument. Using the amended discriminant function, described previously, summary scores for each of the 137 applicants were computed and, based on this score, a prediction was made concerning whether or not the team would have judged the applicant to be More Suitable or Less Suitable for admission to HRCA. See Chart I for items and scoring system used in the computation of the discriminant function. Table 1 describes the distribution of the 137 individuals by Where Post-Tested and by classification of More Suitable or Less Suitable as determined by the amended discriminant function discussed above.

The dependent variables in the present study consist of three components of Life Dissatisfaction: 1) Reaction to Life Events; 2) Generalized Emotional State; and 3) Deprivation in Relation to Former Years. Items from the interview schedule including items from the Powell Lawton Morale Scale and interviewer

CHART I

Independent Variable: Scoring System and Weights Used to Calculate the Discriminant Function to Predict the Team Judgment of Suitability for HRCA (Sherwood and Feldman, 1969).

A. For each person, multiply the person's score on the item by the appropriate weight.

Item	*Score for each item*	*Weight*
Family occupation	1. white collar 2. Other	0.56
Shares bath with non-family member	1. Private or family bath 2. Shares bath with non-family member	0.55
Lives alone (including lives with spouse).	1. Alone 2. Other	0.34
Reads English newspapers	1. English (including combination of English and other) 2. Only other	0.24
Receives financial assistance	1. None 2. Some help	0.24
Modified Rosow Functional Health Scale (4 item scale)	1. Good functional health . . . 4. Poor functional health	0.23
Presently belongs to clubs	1. No 2. Yes	−0.19
Prefers a living situation other than the center	1. Yes 2. Other	0.15
Educational level	1. None 2. Up to 4 years 3. 5-6 years 4. 7-8 years 5. 9-11 years 6. 12 years 7. Some college	−0.14
KATZ-ADL Health Scale (6 item scale)	1. Good functional health . . . 7. Poor functional health	0.12
Lives in nursing home	1. Nursing Home-Hospital 2. Other	0.05
Modified Powell Lawton Morale Scale (20 item scale)	0. Lowest Morale . . . 20. Highest Morale	−0.03
Persons thought of as real friends	1. None 2. 1-5 3. 6-10 4. 11 +	−0.03
Modified Kastenbaum Orientation Scale (8 item scale)	0. Least oriented . . . 24. Most oriented	0.0035

CHART I (Cont.)

B. For each person, add the weighted scores from Step A to determine his discriminate function

$$\sum_{i=1}^{14} (\text{Item} \times \text{Weight})$$

Classify the person as "Best" if his summated weighted score (from Step B) is ≥ 2.780; classify as "Not Best" if summated weighted score is ≤ 2.779.

Note: For the sample in which the discriminant function was derived, the means and standard deviations of the function were as follows:

Rater Classification	$\overline{X}$	S.D.
HRCA More Suitable	= 3.33357	.450736
HRCA Less Suitable	= 2.19386	.580651
Total Sample	= 2.61908	.710426

judgments of psychological well-being which were considered to measure the components of Life Dissatisfaction were factor analyzed. Using the items that loaded on each of the factors obtained, three Likert scales were developed to measure the three components of Life Dissatisfaction. See Chart II for the items and scoring system of each dependent variable.

A three-way analysis of variance repeated measures design was used. One factor or way was the predicted judgment of More Suitable or Less Suitable for HRCA; the second factor was Where Post-Tested (i.e., prior to entry or after entry into the institution); the third factor was the repeated measures factor, Time (i.e., pre-test at one point in time and post-test at a later point in time). Although a three-way analysis of variance provides estimates of the "effects" of each factor considered separately (generally referred to as main effects) these were of only secondary interest in this study. Interest centers here in the interactions (if any) among the factors, and in the one three-way interaction

Table 1. Sample Breakdown by Suitability for HRCA and Sample Group

Suitability for HRCA	*Waiting List Sample*		*Institutional Sample*		
	Number	*Per cent*	*Number*	*Per cent*	
More Suitable	51	54.8	26	59.1	77
Less Suitable	42	45.2	18	40.9	60
	93		44		137

CHART II

Dependent Variables: Scoring for the items of the Components of Life Dissatisfaction.

Reaction to Life Events Scale:

(Add the following 5 items for score.)
(Total score = sum of all items.) Range:5-10
The higher the score the poorer the reaction to life events.

Item	*Score for Each Item*
How much do you feel lonely?	1. Not much 2. A lot
I take things hard.	1. No 2. Yes
I get upset easily.	1. No 2. Yes
I sometimes feel life isn't worth living.	1. No. 2. Yes
I have a lot to be sad about.	1. No. 2. Yes
Grand Mean Score 7.3	

Deprivation in Relation to Former Life Scale:

(Add the following 6 items for score.)
(Total score = sum of all items) Range: 6-12
The higher the score the more the deprivation.

Item	*Score for Each Item*
I am as happy now as I was when I was younger.	1. Yes 2. No
Things keep getting worse as I get older.	1. No 2. Yes
As I get older, things are ______ .	1. Better than I thought they would be 2. Worse - same
People had it better in the old days.	1. No 2. Yes
Little things bother me more this year.	1. No 2. Yes
Life is hard for me most of the time.	1. No 2. Yes
Grand Mean Score 9.14	

Generalized Emotional State Scale:

(Add the following 6 items for score.)
(Total score = sum of all items) Range 6-12
The higher the score the poorer the emotional state.

CHART II (Cont.)

Item		*Score for Each Item*
I am afraid of a lot of things.		1. No 2. Yes
How much do you feel lonely?		1. Not much 2. A lot
How satisfied are you with your life today?		1. Satisfied 2. Not satisfied
Psychological Status: interviewer judgment		1. Adequate functioning 2. Incompetent
Self Assured . . . Insecure: interviewer judgment		1. Self assured, ambivalent 2. Insecure
Emotional State: interviewer judgment		1. Exuberant, even mood 2. Depressed
Grand Mean Score	8.36	

(i.e., Suitability, Time, and Where Post-Tested). The assumptions were as follows: if institutionalization has a differential impact on the two Suitability Groups (that is, if one group adjusts differently *to* institutionalization than the other) then there should be a three-way interaction—that is, the post-test means for any given sub-group, e.g., More Suitable-Post-Tested in the Institution should not be a simple additive function of the three main effects pertaining to that sub-group.

RESULTS

Table 2 presents the data pertaining to this hypothesis. In short, a statistically significant three-way interaction did not appear. However, the data, upon further examination, suggest a finding which may turn out to be even more interesting and significant. For two of the three adjustment measures there was a statistically significant two-way interaction between Suitability and the repeated measure factor Time (i.e., pre-test, post-test). For the third adjustment measure, the results were similar although not statistically significant. As shown in Tables 2 and 3, this two-way interaction is accounted for by the convergence in the scores of the More Suitable and Less Suitable groups over Time. In other words, during the pre-test period the More Suitable group is significantly more dissatisfied with life than the Less Suitable group at the .004 level or better as measured by the three Life Dissatisfaction scales. In the post-test period, however, the life dissatisfaction of the More Suitable group consistently decreases as compared to the life dissatisfaction of the Less Suitable group which either increases or stays the same. In other words, as the groups either become institutionalized or come nearer to institutionalization, the differences between the groups in life dissatisfaction decreases. This pattern manifests itself within each sample (see Table 2) as well as for the combined sample (see Table 3). (Even with this convergence, however, it should be noted that in the post-test period the life dissatisfaction of the More Suitable group is still greater than the life dissatisfaction of the Less Suitable group, although not to a statistically significant degree.)

In any event, the findings from the present study suggest that the amended discriminant function scoring system used for prediction of the team judgment of Suitability for HRCA, is an effective instrument. It is an effective instrument not only for screening purposes but for research purposes as well—it appears to discriminate between kinds of people on the waiting list who are differentially affected by approaching or actual institutionalization.

DISCUSSION

From these findings it would seem that the original analysis model for this study made an assumption which may have been at least misleading, if not unwarranted. It assumed that adjustment *to* institutionalization takes place subsequent to institutionalization. These data at least suggest that the adjustment process may begin *prior* to institutionalization. There is clear evidence, in these data at least, that the More Suitable and Less Suitable groups manifest different pre-test patterns, and this holds whether both tests were administered in the community or one was administered in the community and the other in the institution.

There appear to be two opposing interpretations which might account for these interesting findings. It may be that there are in general two categories of elderly applicants to long term care facilities. One is getting happier, and the other is tending to remain about the same. If this is true, then the findings referred to above can be accounted for by assuming that the discriminant function procedures predicting clinical judgment concerning for whom HRCA was More Suitable or Less Suitable happens to also discriminate between those who are getting happier and those who are remaining the same. Although it may not be, this seems like a rather far-out coincidence. The other interpretation is the one presented here: it rests on the following arguments: First, as is indicated by the results of the previous study, the clinical judgment prediction procedure does discriminate between those who need a place like HRCA from those who do not; or at least between those who need institutionalization more from those who need it less. Second, whether on the conscious or subconscious level, there is recognition of their need on the part of those judged to be more in need of institutionalization. A process of adjustment to institutionalization seems to begin for them at some date prior to actual admission. This process may involve resignation, acceptance, and even the anticipation of benefits of institutionalization. For those judged to be less in need of institutionalization, on the other

Table 2. Mean Scores for Components of Life Dissatisfaction by Suitability for HRCA by Time and by Sample

	Waiting List Sample		*Difference in Mean scores Between More Suitable and Less Suitable Groups*	*Institutional Sample*		*Difference in Mean scores Between More Suitable and Less Suitable Groups*
	More suitable	*Less suitable*		*More suitable*	*Less suitable*	
Life Dissatisfaction Component						
Reaction to Life Events	(N = 51)	(N = 41)		(N = 25)	(N = 18)	
Pre-test	8.10	7.22	.88	7.36	6.89	.47
Post-test	7.76	7.00	.76	7.04	7.06	−.02
Generalized Emotional State	(N = 51)	(N = 42)		(N = 25)	(N = 18)	
Pre-test	9.03	7.93	1.10	8.49	7.55	.94
Post-test	9.16	8.45	.71	8.33	7.94	.39
Deprivation in Relation to Former Life	(N = 50)	(N = 42)		(N - 26)	(N = 18)	
Pre-test	9.83	8.77	.96	9.38	8.39	.99
Post-test	9.86	9.27	.59	8.88	8.69	.19

Table 3. Mean Scores for Components of Life Dissatisfaction by Suitability for HRCA and Time

	More suitable	*Less suitable*	*Differences in Mean scores Between More Suitable and less suitable groups*	*Level of significance*
Life Dissatisfaction Component				
Reaction to Life Events	(N = 76)	(N = 59)		
Pre-test	7.73	7.05	.68	.29
Post-test	7.40	7.03	.37	
Generalized Emotional State	(N = 76)	(N = 60)		
Pre-test	8.76	7.74	1.02	.07
Post-test	8.74	8.20	.54	
Deprivation in Relation to Former Life	(N = 76)	(N = 60)		
Pre-test	9.61	8.58	1.03	.04
Post-test	9.37	8.98	.39	

hand, there is little or no convincing felt need for institutionalization so that the pre-admission period results in either no change or negative changes in terms of life dissatisfaction, as they become institutionalized or approach the time period when they are likely to be offered institutionalization. Confirmation or refutation of the existence of this pre-institutionalization adjustment process (and of its components if its existence appears probable) requires, of course, further research.

The findings from this study suggest the value of applying the Suitability function, which seems meaningfully to separate the sample into two classes of people, for investigations of this type. Had we not classified the groups in this way, we would not have discovered that persons on the waiting list or in the institution are differentially affected by the experience in terms of their life dissatisfaction.

At the very least, the findings from this study suggest that future research attempt to separate a variety of different kinds of effects possibly related to institutionalization: 1) the effects on adjustment, morale, etc., of experiencing events, conditions, personal change leading toward greater need for institutionalization or some alternative to independent living; 2) the effects of formal application to an institution; 3) the effects which occur while waiting for actual admission; 4) the effects of admission; and 5) the effects of institutional life after admission.

REFERENCES

Anderson, Nancy N. Effects of institutionalization on self-esteem. *Journal of Gerontology*, 22(3), 313-17, July 1969.

Lieberman, Morton A., Prock, V., and Tobin, S. Psychological effects of institutionalization. *Journal of Gerontology*, 23(3), 343-53, July 1968.

Sherwood, Sylvia and Feldman, Claire S. The use of easily obtained pre-coded data in screening applicants to a long-term care facility. *The Gerontologist*, 10(3), 182-189, Autumn, 1970, Part I.

Sherwood, Sylvia and Feldman, Claire S. "Development of a Screening Instrument for Assessing Need for Admission to a Long-Term Care Facility for the Aged," paper presented at the 8th International Congress of Gerontology, Washington, D.C., August, 1969.

chapter 5

FROM "WAITING ON THE LIST" TO BECOMING A "NEWCOMER" AND AN "OLDTIMER" IN A HOME FOR THE AGED: TWO STUDIES OF SOCIALIZATION AND ITS IMPACT UPON COGNITIVE FUNCTIONING*

Camilda Weinstock, Ed.D., and Ruth Bennett, Ph.D.

In recent years there has been a growing interest in environmental factors which affect both old and new learning in the aged. Some studies have found that education and institutionalization are related to learning and cognitive functioning in the aged (Granick and Friedman 1967; Comalli, Krus, and Wapner 1965). For the most part, however, poor cognitive functioning in the aged is attributed to organic deterioration associated with the aging process. The strength of this argument usually varies depending on whether a cross-sectional or a longitudinal study was conducted. Most cross-sectional studies of the relationship between age and cognitive functioning have shown that elderly individuals do not compare favorably with younger ones on test performance (Birren and Morrison 1961; Cohen 1962; Riegel 1959). From this, it has been inferred that as the individual progresses from early maturity to old age, his mental faculties deteriorate, especially his ability to learn and remember. However, these findings have not been consistently confirmed by longitudinal studies, some of which have shown that vocabulary and general information tests appear most positively affected by cumulative experience.

Little direct attention has been given to the effects of environmental deprivation or stimulation on cognitive performance. The studies reported here were conducted to determine if some types of social environment were related to the maintenance of a high level of cognitive functioning in the aged. In the first investigation, attention was given to the relations between cognitive performance and social cognition, social isolation, age and mental status in three populations: "newcomers" and "oldtimers" residing in a Jewish home for the aged, and a "waiting list" group residing in the community. The major hypothesis was that aged persons within a stimulating social environment can perform at relatively high levels on tests of cognitive ability as compared with their socially deprived counterparts. Age, per se, was *not* thought to be the factor accounting for poor cognitive functioning. The second study is a follow-up and will be reported separately below.

*The first of the two studies reported here is based in part on data from a 1968 Ed.D. thesis from the Department of Developmental Psychology, Teachers College, Columbia University, supported in part by a predoctoral fellowship from the New York State Department of Education. An earlier version of the paper was presented at the annual meetings of the Gerontological Society, in Denver, 1968. The second study was reported at the International Congress of Gerontology, Washington, D.C., in 1969.

FIRST STUDY

Sample

Sixty persons, over 65 years of age, comparable on background characteristics such as age, sex, education, religion and place of birth, and differing only as to place and length of residence, were interviewed. Two thirds were female, one third were male. More than half of the total sample was in the 80-89 year old range. Oldtimers had a mean age of 83.7, waiting list subjects, 79.8, and newcomers, 79.3. Forty percent of the total sample had had at least some high school education. Over forty percent of the total sample were native-born Americans. The newcomers had the highest proportion of foreign-born subjects. The sample was divided for place and length of residence as follows: twenty waiting list subjects residing in the community, twenty newcomers to the Home and twenty oldtimers whose length of residence in the Home was more than one year. Newcomers were selected by the authors and included twenty consecutive new admissions to the Home who were English-speaking and could complete the interview. Oldtimers and waiting list subjects were selected by staff members of the Home's social service department according to their estimate of the subjects' fluency in English and intactness.

Method

A standard interview lasting approximately one hour was administered. It contained the following indices:

1. The Adulthood Isolation Index, which is a measure of the extent of lifetime social contacts with family, friends, work and organizations.
2. Past Month Isolation Index, which is a measure of number of social contacts outside the institution in the month prior to the interview.
3. Three Wechsler Adult Intelligence Scale (*WAIS*) subtests: Information, containing twenty questions measuring basic knowledge of topics ranging from names of composers to the colors in the flag; Comprehension, containing fourteen items designed to measure the ability to combine information into new forms; and Similarities, which is a measure of conceptualization with thirteen items of paired association.
4. Socialization Index, which is a measure of the amount of information learned about life in the Home, consisting of fifteen questions about formal procedures and norms in the Home such as "What kinds of activities are available during the day?"
5. Mental Status Schedule, which is an instrument containing 350 items worded for true-false judgments of current psychopathology based on data collected during the interview.

Means and standard deviations of total scores were obtained for all indices. Pearson correlation coefficients were computed to demonstrate correlations between major independent and dependent variables.

Findings

Table 1 shows the distribution of means of *WAIS* test scores for waiting list subjects, newcomers and oldtimers. Mean scores on all the *WAIS* subtests were higher for the

TABLE 1
Mean Scores on *WAIS* Subtests and Socialization Index in Waiting List, Newcomer and Oldtimer Groups*

Mean *WAIS* Scores	Waiting List Group	Newcomers	Oldtimers
Information	13.10	15.00	13.55
Similarities	5.95	7.40	6.35
Comprehension	13.50	15.65	16.45
WAIS Total	32.55	38.05	36.35
Socialization Index	10.10	18.50	20.30

* Chi square were computed for differences found among groups for all tests. They were as follows:

WAIS information:	2.73 p < .10
WAIS similarities:	3.16 p < .10
WAIS comprehension:	6.13 p < .02
Total *WAIS*:	9.57 p < .01
Socialization Index:	64.56 p < .001

resident groups than for the waiting list group, though these differences were not significant. The newcomers' scores on *WAIS* total and on all *WAIS* subtests with the exception of *WAIS* comprehension were higher than those of both the waiting list group and oldtimers. Differences in mean *WAIS* total were significant at the .01 level across groups. Newcomers seemed to perform best possibly because they were in the process of being socialized; oldtimers seemed to have reached a learning plateau; and waiting list persons performed worst perhaps because they were most deprived of stimulation.

The mean scores on the Socialization Index for waiting list subjects, newcomers and oldtimers are also shown in Table 1. As might have been anticipated, residents as a group obtained markedly higher socialization scores than persons on the waiting list. The waiting list group, despite having passed through the admission procedure which included considerable interaction with the Home's personnel, was largely unaware of norms and practices current in the Home. The mean Socialization score for the waiting list group was 10.1 out of a possible score of 30 and was the lowest of the three groups. Oldtimers obtained higher Socialization scores than newcomers; their mean was 20.3 in contrast to a mean of 18.5 obtained by newcomers. These differences were significant at the .001 level across the three groups. Unlike the pattern of scores on the *WAIS* subtests, on which newcomers obtained the highest scores, Socialization scores appeared to reflect increments in experience obtained with increased tenure in the Home. The pattern of scores also indicates that the Socialization measure and the *WAIS* measures, with the possible exception of *WAIS* comprehension, were independent of one another.

The correlations between scores on all *WAIS* subtests and scores on the Socialization Index are shown in Table 2. For newcomers, correlation coefficients for the relations between all *WAIS* subtests and the Socialization Index were significantly higher than for those of the other two groups. The correlation coefficients were as follows: .77 for information and socialization, .51 for similarities and socialization, .78 for comprehension and socialization, and .74 for *WAIS* total and socialization. Newcomers appeared to be so highly involved in a salient learning experience that they performed better on all measures of cognitive skills. The awareness brought about by involvement in the socialization process seemed to "spill over" to performance on the other tests. The converse did not seem to be true, that is, good past cognitive performance did not seem to account for high Socialization scores. All groups had had a similar high level of education; accordingly, they should have performed similarly at the outset. In point of fact, they did not. Moreover, level of education did not correlate with either *WAIS* subtests or the Socialization measure.

The data also showed that in residents as a group, socialization related most to the measure most like it, namely, comprehension, and least to the measure most unlike it, namely, similarities. This was most evident, of course, in the newcomer group. Thus, if residents were stimulated by involvement in the socialization process they were more likely to demonstrate this stimulation by a high level of general comprehension and information, not just about life in the Home but about the world outside.

Correlation coefficients among *WAIS* subtests and total *WAIS* scores for all three groups are shown in Table 3. All correlation coefficients were significant at the .01 level. However, for the most part they were highest in the newcomer group, probably having been affected by the ongoing process of socialization, thus, again showing the "spill-over" effect. The factors of age, isolation and mental status were also investigated to determine their effects on cognitive performance. Age per se, did not relate to poor cognitive functioning. Although the waiting list sample was younger than the total resident sample, they did not perform as well on any tests. In general, when groups were divided at their median ages and younger subjects compared with older ones, the older ones performed

TABLE 2
Correlation Coefficients between *WAIS* Subtests and Socialization Index for the Waiting List, Newcomer and Oldtimer Groups

	Socialization Index		
WAIS Tests	Waiting List Group	Newcomers	Oldtimers
Information	.45*	.77**	.60**
Similarities	.51*	.51*	.18
Comprehension	.57**	.78**	.65**
WAIS Total	.56**	.74**	.58**

* $p < .05$
** $p < .01$

TABLE 3
Correlation Coefficients among *WAIS* Subtests and Total *WAIS* Scores for Waiting List, Newcomer and Oldtimer Groups*

	Waiting List Group				Newcomers				Oldtimers			
WAIS Tests	WAIS info.	WAIS simil.	WAIS com-pre.	Total WAIS	WAIS info.	WAIS simil.	WAIS com-pre.	Total WAIS	WAIS info.	WAIS simil.	WAIS com-pre.	Total WAIS
Information	1.00	.79	.74	.94	1.00	.74	.94	.95	1.00	.59	.85	.92
Similarities	.79	1.00	.61	.90	.74	1.00	.80	.89	.59	1.00	.60	.77
Comprehension	.74	.61	1.00	.86	.94	.80	1.00	.97	.85	.60	1.00	.93
WAIS total	.94	.90	.86	1.00	.95	.89	.97	1.00	.92	.77	.93	1.00

* All correlation coefficients shown in this table were significant at $p < .01$ or less.

TABLE 4
Distribution of Mean Scores on *WAIS* Subtests and Socialization Index for Above and Below Median Age Subjects in Waiting List, Newcomer and Oldtimer Groups

	Waiting List		Newcomers		Oldtimers	
WAIS Test Scores	Old (*a*)	Young (*b*)	Old (*c*)	Young (*d*)	Old (*e*)	Young (*f*)
Information	14.11	12.27	16.81	12.77	13.0	14.1
Similarities	5.44	6.36	8.63	5.88	5.3	7.4
Comprehension	13.88	12.27	16.72	12.88	14.5	18.4
WAIS total	33.44	31.76	43.36	31.55	32.8	40.9
Socialization Index	10.44	9.81	20.18	16.44	20.2	20.4

(*a*) Ages 80 and above
(*b*) Ages 79 and below
(*c*) Ages 81 and above
(*d*) Ages 80 and below
(*e*) Ages 85 and above
(*f*) Ages 84 and below

better (see Table 4). This was particularly true of older residents in general but especially of the older newcomers, who were found to have higher scores than the young waiting list subjects. Possibly this indicated that the older members of the samples benefitted most from environmental stimulation.

Another factor thought to affect cognitive performance was that of social isolation. We expected the waiting list group to be significantly more socially isolated than the resident groups, and thought social isolation might have explained the obtained results. However, this was definitely not the case. There were no significant correlations between isolation and *WAIS* subtests. Furthermore, the waiting list subjects were not significantly more isolated than the other two groups. Since no significant differences were found among groups with regard to either adulthood or present isolation, further analysis attempted to illustrate the pattern of isolation for the three groups. Four categories of isolation were constructed as follows: (*a*) *Lifelong Isolates*—those subjects who had below median scores on both the Adulthood and Past Month Isolation Indices. (*b*) *Old Age Isolates* (Involuntary Isolates)—those subjects who had above median scores on Adulthood Isolation Index but below median scores on the Past Month Isolation Index. (*c*) *Old Age Non-Isolates*—those subjects who scored below the median on the Adulthood Isolation Index but above the median on Past Month Isolation. (*d*) *Lifelong Non-Isolates*—those subjects who scored above the median on both the Adulthood Isolation and Past Month Isolation Indices.

When subjects were divided according to these patterns of isolation, there were some interesting differences. Table 5 shows the relationship between patterns of isolation and cognitive performance in the newcomer, oldtimer and waiting list groups. Cognitive functioning was affected by pattern of isolation but not in the same manner for all goups. Old age or involuntary isolates were found to have the lowest scores on *WAIS* subtests within the waiting list and oldtimer groups. These subjects seemed to suffer those effects of social isolation which are concomitant with aging. However, in the newcomer group those who had been involuntarily isolated performed very well on *WAIS* tests. In newcomers, the involuntary isolates actually performed better on most cognitive and socialization measures than did the lifelong non-isolates in the other groups.

In the oldtimer group, involuntary isolates performed significantly worse on all tests than did any others in their group. However, even involuntarily isolated oldtimers performed better than involuntarily isolated waiting list persons. Prolonged institutionalization seems to have had a positive effect as demonstrated by the fact that of all lifelong isolates, those in the oldtimer group did best. From these findings it may be inferred that social contacts are as necessary as stimulating learning experiences for the maintenance of a high level of cognitive functioning.

As for mental status, cognitive differences among groups could not be explained in terms of scores obtained on the Mental Status Schedule (*MSS*). The data showed little evidence of psychopathology among the three groups, Moreover, no pattern of correlations with cognitive performance could be found.

However, some mention should be made of the relation between anxiety and cognitive performance. It seemed reasonable to expect the waiting list group to experience the most anxiety during the test-taking situation because (*a*) they may have believed their test performance would influence entry into the Home, (*b*) they were in the process of becoming uprooted and changing their life patterns, and (*c*) they were undergoing a new and perhaps frightening test-taking experience. That such anxiety was present was indicated by their mean *MSS* score on the Feelings-Concerns Scale (the anxiety subscale of the *MSS*) which was slightly higher for waiting list subjects than for the other two groups.

None of the correlations between the Feelings-Concerns Scale and *WAIS* subtest scores were found to be significant. In fact, the correlated scores of the waiting list group paralleled those found for the newcomer group. It does not seem likely that if anxiety were accounting for poor cognitive functioning it would have differentially affected the newcomers and waiting list subjects such that the former would have performed best, and the latter worst. Moreover, in the oldtimer group, the more anxious they were, the better their cognitive performance. Since anxiety did not seem to work in any systematic fashion across groups, it seems reasonable to conclude tenetatively that it played no major role in cognitive performance.

TABLE 5
Mean Test Scores According to Patterns of Isolation for Waiting List, Newcomer and Oldtimer Groups

	Waiting List Group				Newcomers				Oldtimers			
WAIS Tests	Life-long Isol.	Old Age Isol.	Old Age Non-Isol.	Life-long Non-Isol.	Life-long Isol.	Old Age Isol.	Old Age Non-Isol.	Life-long Non-Isol.	Life-long Isol.	Old Age Isol.	Old Age Non-Isol.	Life-long Non-Isol.
Information	13.6	8.8		15.0	8.3	18.5	17.5	14.5	12.0	11.0	17.0	16.2
Similarities	4.3	3.8		7.9	1.5	7.3	9.3	10.2	5.9	5.2	11.0	5.4
Comprehension	13.1	9.8		16.1	9.8	17.8	17.0	16.5	15.3	13.0	23.0	19.6
WAIS total	32.1	22.3		39.0	19.5	43.5	43.8	41.2	34.6	29.2	51.0	39.2
Socialization Index	9.8	8.5		10.9	15.0	21.0	18.5	18.3	19.1	18.8	21.3	27.0
Total Number	9	4		7	4	6	4	6	7	5	3	5

DISCUSSION

The hypothesis that old people, involved in a stimulating environment, would perform best on tests of cognitive abilities was supported. Residents of a home for aged obtained higher mean *WAIS* total and subtest scores than their waiting list counterparts. In general, newcomers obtained higher scores than both oldtimers and waiting list persons on tests of cognitive ability. The Home seem to provide the type of environment which sustained a high level of cognitive performance. These findings seem best explained by a "disuse" model of cognitive functioning which holds that unless cognitive skills are put to use, they tend to be "forgotten" or possibly lost. Opportunities to put them to use in the Home were many and varied. Newcomers were introduced to a social setting which required new learning on a daily basis. They were actively involved in the process of learning the role of a new member of the Home. To learn this role it was necessary for them to be aware of, and accumulate information about, the norms and expectations of the Home. Some of this information was communicated to them through talks with social service workers and through printed material sent prior to entry, as evidenced by the fact that waiting list subjects knew some of the rules of the institution. In the main, learning about the role of becoming an institutional resident occurred through a process of daily interaction between newly admitted residents and oldtimers within the Home. This communication process necessitated continual social interaction with other residents, some of whom acted as role models as well as teachers. Staff members also were in constant touch with newcomers, keeping them alert to expectations for behavior, observing them closely and repeatedly sanctioning them. Newcomers were seldom left to their own devices or allowed to sit idle; they were constantly active and involved, possibly to avoid rejection by their peers or admonition by staff members.

Age, isolation and mental status did not explain the obtained results.

This study has the following limitations:

1. The aged individuals studied were neither a random sample of aged persons in general nor of aged persons residing in the Home studied. Also, as is obvious, the samples were very small. Therefore, the findings cannot be generalized to other aged individuals.

2. The Home studied cannot be said to be representative of homes for aged. It seems important to note that although their institutionalization seems to work favorably for the newcomers to this home, no conclusions should be drawn that institutionalization per se is the solution to maintenance of good cognitive functioning in the aged.

3. Some of the indices used in this study, particularly those of social isolation, were crude in the sense that they focused on number of social contacts rather than on any measures of intensity or frequency of contact. Thus, the findings that residents experience about the same number of social contact losses as did the community group, indicated that the isolation measures did not discriminate the two groups.

The following implications may be drawn from this research. First, cognitive functioning of aged individuals seems to be affected by social milieu; cognitive impairment may be related to the negative social concomitants of aging, rather than the aging process itself. Second, a home for aged which is concerned about maintaining good cognitive functioning in its residents should direct its attention to the socialization process for newly admitted residents in particular, and for all residents in general. If meaningful social interactions and learning experiences were provided throughout a resident's length of tenure in an institution, oldtimers might not show any cognitive decrements. Third, aged persons residing in the community might not show cognitive impairment if exposed to stimulating social learning experiences.

SECOND STUDY

One year after the initial study, a follow-up was conducted at the same institution. This longitudinal extension tested the general hypothesis that the socialization process is a salient, highly stimulating learning experience which positively affects other cognitive processes. Therefore, we expected to find that a former waiting list person when interviewed in his new status as a newcomer resident of the Home would show improvement on tests of cognitive ability. We thought former newcomers might show signs of decline. We did not know what to predict for oldtimers grown even older.

Sample

The original sample had been divided for place and length of residence as follows: twenty waiting list subjects who resided in the community, twenty newcomers to the home whose length of residence was under two months (with an average of less than two weeks) and twenty oldtimers whose length of residence in the Home ranged from one to eighteen years with an average of two years. The newcomer group consisted of twenty consecutive new admissions to the Home who were English-speaking and could complete the interview. Oldtimers and waiting list subjects in the original sample were selected by members of the Home's social service department staff according to their estimate of the subjects' fluency in English and their intactness. The present follow-up sample includes all surviving subjects from the original sample whose physical and mental condition permitted their participation in an hour long interview. The survivors constituted a group of twenty-eight females and twelve males (the original sample of sixty had forty-one females and nineteen males). There were twelve surviving former waiting list persons, newcomers at the time of the second study. Seven persons from the original twenty waiting list persons were deceased and one had a serious heart condition which prevented her from being tested. There were fourteen former newcomers surviving, oldtimers in the duration of the second study. Four of the original twenty newcomers were deceased and two had become senile and could not be retested. There were fourteen former oldtimers who were given second interviews, and these oldtimers were "older oldtimers" at the time of the second study. Three of the original sample of twenty were deceased and three were senile and non-interviewable. Mean chronological ages of the groups were 79.1 years for former waiting list persons, 80.1 for former newcomers and 85 for former oldtimers.

The percentages of resident and waiting list subjects for age, sex, education and birthplace in both past and present sample are shown in Table 6.

Method

A standard interview lasting approximately one hour was administered. It was identical to that given to the original sample in the first study. Means and standard deviations of total scores were obtained for all indices. Pearson correlation coefficients were computed to demonstrate correlations between major independent and dependent variables.

TABLE 6
Percentages of Subjects with Selected Background Characteristics

Background Characteristic	Waiting List N = 20		Newcomers N = 20		Oldtimers N = 20		Total N = 60	
	Time 1	Time 2	Time 1	Time 2	Time 1	Time 2	Time 1	Time 2
Age								
65-69	5	5	10	10			5	5
70-79	50	20	25	10	15	15	30	15
80-89	35	35	65	50	70	40	57	42
90+	10				15	15	8	5
Non-survivors		40		30		30		33
Total	100	100	100	100	100	100	100	100
Sex								
Female	90	50	65	50	50	40	68	47
Male	10	10	35	20	50	30	32	20
Non-survivors		40		30		30		33
Total	100	100	100	100	100	100	100	100
Education								
Elementary School	55	30	55	35	65	45	58	37
High School	45	30	45	35	35	25	42	30
Non-survivors		40		30		30		33
Total	100	100	100	100	100	100	100	100
Birthplace								
United States	45	30	30	25	55	45	43	33
Eastern Europe	10	10	55	35	15	10	27	20
Central and Western Europe	45	20	15	10	30	15	30	14
Non-survivors		40		30		30		33
Total	100	100	100	100	100	100	100	100

Results

The mean scores on the *WAIS* subtests for each group at each time are shown in Table 7. It is clear that the former waiting list group is the only group to show a gain in all *WAIS* measures. Former newcomers who had been performing at the highest level of all groups on the first interview continued to demonstrate their superiority on test scores one year later, with only minor losses over time. Former oldtimers showed the most precipitous, general drop in scores on all *WAIS* subtests. However, the oldtimers continued to show some evidence of maintenance of cognitive functioning by their gain in socialization scores. Unlike the pattern of scores on the *WAIS* subtests, socialization scores appear to reflect increments in experience obtained with increased tenure in the Home. These scores show improvement through all groups, but the gains diminish, perhaps indicating that there is little more to be learned.

Table 8 shows the percentage of gains and losses in *WAIS* scores for each group over time. Time 1 and Time 2 scores were compared for each subject on each test. Any change of more than one point in score was scored as a loss or gain. Score changes from Time 1 to Time 2 of one or no points were counted as the same.

The *WAIS* information test scores showed the most stability for all three groups.

Similarities scores showed the highest percentage of gains for the waiting list group but almost half of both newcomers and oldtimers showed drops in similarity scores. One-third of the waiting list gained in their comprehension scores in the time they were institutional residents. Over half of the oldtimers, however, showed losses of more than one point on retest. One-half of the waiting list population showed gains in total *WAIS* score and only one-third showed losses. Sixty-four per cent of the newcomers either gained points or maintained total *WAIS* score on retest. However, almost three-quarters of the oldtimers showed losses on total *WAIS* scores over time. In general, effects of environmental stimulation seemed most evident for the former waiting list group who had become newcomers and least for oldtimers.

The factors of age, isolation and mental status were investigated to determine their effects on cognitive performance. Within groups, age per se did not relate to gains or losses on *WAIS* subtests. On retest oldtimers showed greatest losses, but this was evidently unrelated to chronological age because age cohorts in the waiting list and newcomer groups did not show such losses. Oldtimers' length of residence in the old age home did not relate to gains and losses in *WAIS* scores. When the scores of oldtimers in

TABLE 7
Mean Scores on *WAIS* subtests and Socialization Index for Studies 1 and 2 for Survivors Only
($N = 40$)

WAIS Subtest	Waiting List Group Study 1	Waiting List Group Study 2	Newcomers Study 1	Newcomers Study 2	Oldtimers Study 1	Oldtimers Study 2
Information	13.1	13.6	17.1	16.5	14.0	12.8
Similarities	6.6	8.1	8.6	9.4	6.9	4.8
Comprehension	13.9	14.9	17.1	16.5	17.0	14.1
WAIS total	33.7	36.6	42.8	42.5	37.9	31.6
Socialization Index	10.1	22.8	18.5	22.8	20.3	22.9

TABLE 8
Percentage of Subjects Whose *WAIS* Scores Changed From Time 1 to Time 2

WAIS subtests		Waiting List Group	Newcomers	Oldtimers
Information	% up	25	14	14
	% same	50	50	50
	% down	25	36	36
Similarities	% up	42	36	21
	% same	50	21	36
	% down	8	43	43
Comprehension	% up	33	28	7
	% same	42	28	36
	% down	25	44	57
WAIS Total	% up	50	36	14
	% same	17	28	14
	% down	33	36	72

TABLE 9
Mean Total *WAIS* Scores According to Patterns of Isolation for Study 1 and Study 2 for All Groups

	Waiting List Group		Newcomers		Oldtimers	
	Study 1	Study 2	Study 1	Study 2	Study 1	Study 2
Lifelong Isolates	36.8	43.6	47.0	46.5	42.5	35.5
Old Age Isolates	10.0	16.0	32.3	29.3	49.0	33.0
Old Age Non-Isolates	16.0	14.0	46.3	37.3	34.3	32.0
Lifelong Non-Isolates	38.8	38.4	48.3	50.3	35.0	29.7

residence five years or less were compared with those in residence over five years, it was found that 75 percent of the short term residents had suffered losses in total *WAIS* and 66 percent of the long term residents has shown losses. However, the average amount of loss was higher for those residents who had been in the old age home five years or less than it was for those who had survived institutionalization longer than five years. It seems evident that the old age home does not provide a stimulating environment for everyone for all time.

Cognitive functioning was affected by patterns of isolation but not in the same manner for all groups (Table 9). All oldtimers demonstrated a drop in mean total *WAIS* score; old age isolates showed the most precipitous drop. However, in the former waiting list group those who had been isolated performed very well on *WAIS* retesting. All isolates from the former waiting list actually performed better as newcomers on most cognitive measures. This had been true of the newcomer group in the first study. At that time, in newcomers, the involuntary isolates actually performed better on cognitive and socialization measures than did the lifelong non-isolates in the other groups. The implication is that isolates benefitted most from the environmental stimulation. Looking at the newcomer group, we can see that anyone with a history of isolation shows a drop in total *WAIS* score. Only the lifelong non-isolates continue to improve. Presumably, again, the Home seems to provide the initial force for maintenance and/or improvement in intellectual functioning. However, with time, this stimulation diminishes, and there is overall decline for all except those with a strong life history of social interaction. As for mental status, cognitive differences among groups could not be explained in terms of scores obtained on the Mental Status Schedule (*MSS*). The data showed little evidence of psychopathology among the three groups. No pattern of correlations with cognitive performance could be found.

Discussion

It had been hypothesized that a stimulating environment which provides salient new learning situations, and which is supportive through peer and staff social interaction, would positively affect performance on a test of cognitive functioning. This hypothesis was supported. Those individuals who were engaged in the socialization process in order to adapt to the role of newcomer showed gains in cognitive performance on retest. Former newcomers, who were beginning to settle into and accept oldtimer status showed some signs of loss in cognitive functioning. Oldtimers showed the greatest percentage of loss in scores on all *WAIS* subtests of any of the three groups. Furthermore, they seemed most negatively affected by social isolation. Former waiting list persons, such as new residents, stimulated by new experiences, were socially and cognitively alert. But the old age home evidently does not continue to provide this stimulation on a long term basis.

Institutionalization affects people differently. After about one year of residence the transition from newcomer to oldtimer status is achieved, and the lack of challenge and new roles and relationships becomes evident: newcomer status provides residents with daily stimulation and tangible goals, whereas oldtimer status–although not without privileges–provides fewer incentives, since the environment and the residents have stabilized to a great extent. Using a longitudinal design, this study has confirmed earlier findings of our cross-sectional study and those of Lieberman, Prock and Tobin (1968), and Anderson (1964). All these studies demonstrated mixed efforts, negative and positive, of institutionalization. However, our longitudinal study has enabled us to pinpoint in time the onset of these negative effects. Presumably, they can be offset with environmental manipulation.

Is the improved performance of the former waiting list group a function of the increased stimulation provided during the socialization process. Or is it a mark of their greater fitness for survival? In point of fact, more former waiting list persons died between Time 1 and Time 2 than was true for the other two groups. However, if survivorship alone accounted for improved performance, then the former newcomers who supposedly represented the most "fit" at Time 1 should have continued to improve cognitively with continued institutionalization. This was clearly not the case; while more of them survived, more of them declined in cognitive performance. Again, let us point out that the environmental stimulation of the socialization process and the impact of institutionalization are temporal variables.

An applicant can anticipate, then prepare for, and finally involve himself in the socialization process–learning and practicing where to go, what to do, whom to meet, when to speak–as a new resident. Performance brings the rewards of acceptance by staff, residents and family. Once orientation is accomplished, continued daily participation, e.g., volunteering for certain privilege jobs, can help newcomers further establish themselves. However, eventually there fail to be new rewards and experiences to prevent the monotony of passing days and the realization that these days are among one's last. Studies by Leiberman and Lakin (1963) and Hadley (1963) have stressed the debilitating and deteriorative aspects of institutionalization of the aged. Programs in institutions seek to introduce work-like recreation activities to attempt to maintain some semblance of former life patterns. But our data seem to point to the need for some further thought about institutional programming.

If meaningful learning experiences, positive milestones, were provided throughout a resident's length of tenure in an institution, then oldtimers might show fewer cognitive decrements. Furthermore, such deterioration as takes place in waiting list persons, which seems to be overcome by the initial impact of newcomer status, might be avoided altogether through concerted community effort to provide the social and intellectual support and prevent role loss experienced by the non-institutionalized elderly.

REFERENCES

Anderson, N. N. Social activity, self-conception and institutionalization of older people. Paper presented at 7th annual meeting of Gerontological Society, October 29, 1964, Minneapolis, Minnesota.

Bennett, R. Distinguishing characteristics of the aging from a sociological viewpoint. *Journal of the American Geriatric Society*, 1968, *16*, 2, 127-135.

Birren, J. E., & Morrison, D. F. Analysis of the WAIS subtests in relation to age and education *Journal of Gerontology*, 1961, *16*, 4, 363-369.

Cohen, C. S. Research on mental abilities and aging. *Adult Education*, 1962, *12*, 165-172.

Comalli, P. E., Krus, D. M., & Wapner, S. Cognitive functioning in two groups of aged: one institutionalized, the other living in the community. *Journal of Gerontology*, 1967, *20*, 1, 9-13.

Granick, S., & Friedman, A. S. The effect of education on the decline of psychometric test performance with age. *Journal of Gerontology*, 1967, *22*, 191-195.

Hadley, R. G. Psychological changes in institutional residents. Research Project, Domicilary Psychological Service, V. A. Center, Los Angeles, California, Mimeograph, June, 1963.

Lieberman, M. A., & Kakin, M. On becoming an institutionalized aged person. In R. H. Williams, C. Tibbetts and W. Donahue (Eds.), *Processes of Aging*, Vol. 1. New York: Atherton Press, 1963.

Lieberman, M. A., Prock, V. N., & Tobin, S. S. Psychological effects of institutionalization. *Journal of Gerontology*, 1968, *23*, 343-353.

Riegel, K. F. A study of verbal achievements of older persons. *Journal of Gerontology*, 1959, *14*, 4, 453-456.

chapter 6

AN EXPLORATORY STUDY OF PATTERNS OF SOCIAL INTERACTION, ORGANIZATION, AND FACILITY DESIGN IN THREE NURSING HOMES[1]

Lorraine Hiatt Snyder, M.A.

INTRODUCTION

> One really learns only from people, and friends are people who put you in contact with so much of the world. They help you to form–to discover–yourself. So it's important in a selfish way to have friends to discover what you really are. A real friend gives you the occasion to express yourself. Some need a large number of friends; for some, a few are sufficient.
>
> –René Dubos at age 70
> (Freese, 1971, p. 59)

Although most social gerontologists and practitioners in the field agree that interpersonal relations among the aging are generally beneficial (Bell, 1967; Lawton, 1968; Mason, 1954; Anderson, 1965; Donahue, 1966; Carp, 1967), research has had very little to report about how to promote or encourage social interaction among the aged. We are particularly naive about creating a social environment for those older persons who live in total institutions such as in a nursing home (Stotsky, 1970; Lawton, 1970, 1971; Sommer, 1969; Goffman, 1961). There are at least three means through which one might work to promote

[1] This paper is based on the author's Master of Arts thesis (Snyder, 1972). The data were collected as part of a larger study titled, "An evaluation of an existing environmental interface with the aging person." The thesis was supported by a College of Human Ecology Overhead Grant # 350. The larger project was funded by Hatch # 407 from the New York State Agriculture Experiment Station, Cornell University, Ithaca, New York.

social interaction: management and policy implementation, individual behavior, and social and physical environment. Since the three are interrelated they might best be examined together.

In an exploratory investigation of three extended care facilities in New York State, an effort has been made to study the relationship of environmental design, management, the individual, and social interaction. This paper focuses on factors that promote or deter social interaction. The findings are empirically grounded and should be studied in other settings to determine their general applicability.

REVIEW OF PERTINENT LITERATURE

Previous research on social interaction among the aged has been of three major types. Some researchers have compared and contrasted the institutionalized with the non-institutionalized aged individual. These studies have generally demonstrated that less social interaction takes place in the nursing home or home for the aged than among comparable people living in the general community (Lipman, 1967; Scott, 1955). Retirement communities, which tend to serve a more able population of elderly persons, do not seem to deter social relations. According to several reports, social interaction and morale have increased after living in the retirement community (Carp, 1967; Donahue, 1966; Anderson, 1965). Research findings on social relations among independent aged may not be directly applicable to dependent nursing home residents.

A second type of writing and research has attempted to explain the reasons for low levels of interaction among the aged. These studies include the theoretical and empirical works of Cumming and Henry (Cumming and Henry, 1961; Cumming, 1964), as well as studies by Tec and Granick (1959-1960), Bennett (1968), and Tissue and Wells (1971). These researchers suggest that low levels of social interaction may reflect one's previous life style as well as one's present age and status. Physical and sensory characteristics of the aged have been related to lower levels of social interaction by several researchers (Derrick and Kagan, 1967; DeLong, 1970; Bergman, 1971). Due to decrements in vision, hearing, and mobility, the aged individual may find social relations a great physical effort.

Research on the relationship between the aged individual and his physical setting has also shed some light on social behavior. On a macroscopic level, researchers such as Rosow (1965) and Messer (1967) have found that aged persons in a community of other elderly are more socially outgoing than older persons living in an age integrated community. These findings are, however, tempered by other characteristics of the individuals involved. Several social scientists have observed perpetually lower levels of interaction among aged residents of an institution (Wax, 1962; Stotsky, 1970; Zinberg and Kaufman, 1963). They offer several reasons for this phenomenon including: illness, institutional repetitiveness, and desire to identify with and hence interact with younger, stronger individuals. Lawton (1971) has summarized their observations, commenting that institutions afford high rates of encounter but low levels of social interaction.

Both Lawton (1970) and Sommer (1970) have proposed some physical arrangements that appear to promote social relations in the institutions that they studied. Lawton reports that circular arrangements of rooms around the nursing station promotes social interaction between both staff and residents and among the residents themselves. He further notes that residents respond better when they have their own private area as well as a communal meeting space (Lawton, et al., 1970). Although Lawton's findings on the relationship between privacy and social interaction are based on psychiatric aged patients, they coincide with DeLong's observations (1970) on a wider range of elderly institutionalized individuals. Sommer (1969) suggests that tables be made available in dayrooms of homes for the aged so that residents have a reason to draw together. He notes that the conventional side-by-side seating around the periphery of a room does not appear to promote conversation due to limitations on eye contact.

These studies are primarily suggestive rather than prescriptive. Few projects have centered on more than one institution or taken a constellation of variables into account. There is no empirical evidence to demonstrate that results from one type of housing or from one group of institutionalized aged should be meaningfully generalized to others. These difficulties reflect both the newness of this type of research and of the methods employed.

The practitioner or nursing home administrator who is attempting to conscientiously develop his facility finds himself in a real quandary. He must live up to a Federal Code (if he has an extended care facility) mandating that a standard dayroom be "attractively furnished" and "of adequate size for patient dining, diversional and social activities (U.S., 1966)." Researchers offer few concrete prescriptions because they simply do not have the data. The owner, board of directors, or administrator has no set of principles or guidelines to which he may turn for direction in actual practice. A systematic program of research offers a means of assisting these decision makers. This research may also provide an objective or neutral basis for code development.

DESCRIPTION OF RESEARCH

In the state of New York alone, there are 620 certified extended care facilities (American Nursing Home Association, 1971). This study centers on merely three. Selection of these three facilities was based on several criteria:

1. Certification–All facilities were to be certified as extended care facilities receiving Medicare patients. Extended care facilities were chosen due to their stated goal of rehabilitation and more comparable available services (all else being equal).

2. Proximity to Research Base of Operations–Facilities within central New York were chosen due to the logistics of traveling and of lodging the field workers.
3. Management Stability–Facilities which had had time to adjust to the present management were sought because the administrator would have had more time to put his ideas into practice.
4. Size–Based on projections of size for future nursing homes, nursing homes of at least 100 beds were considered more appropriate for the study.
5. Comparability of Date of Construction–To reduce comparisons between "new" and "old," facilities of comparable date of construction (mid to late 1960's) were selected from the final pool.
6. Sponsorship–For purposes of comparison, facilities of each one of the three types of sponsorship (private, voluntary, and public) were sought.

No claim is made that the three facilities eventually selected are representative of all nursing homes or of all extended care facilities, or of nursing homes of each sponsorship type.

Method

Sommer (1969) has suggested that research which is geared toward a study of the physical, social, and individual environment be based on a variety of data gathering methods. Following his recommendations, several techniques were developed for use in this study:

1. Administrators' Interviews–Each nursing home administrator was interviewed to determine the background of his facility and his ideas on design and planning.
2. Physical Data on Setting–Descriptions of the physical environment, including inventories of room furnishings and appointments, were systematically recorded. Typical rooms in each facility were measured in order to make uniform floor plans. These floor plans were then used in conjunction with the observation forms.
3. Visual Records–Photographs were taken in each area studied of the room itself and of specific items of interest.
4. Systematic Observation–Systematic observations were made of the residents as they occupied and interacted in each social area.
5. Resident Interviews–Guided interviews were conducted with 25% of the residents in each facility. Due to the fact that many residents were either ill or unable to communicate, these interviews are neither random nor necessarily representative of all residents. Interviews were used as a basis for highlighting environmental incongruities as well as for determining patterns of daily life and facility use.

6. Staff Interviews–Staff members were informally queried about their observations on design functionality and resident use of various rooms.

The observational technique used is based on some procedures termed "behavior mapping (Ittelson, 1967; Barker and Barker, 1961; Ittelson, et al., 1970; Snyder, 1972)." Simple recording forms were developed so that observers would collect the following data (among other items):

1. role of the users or room occupants
2. range of activities and role categories of participants
3. patterns of room use and room avoidance
4. duration of room use and activity occurrence
5. occurrence of social contact.

The findings reported are based primarily on the behavior records resulting from these observations.

Procedure

Six field workers participated in a week long training period and a series of observations and interviews at a home for the aged prior to collecting data for the present study. The agenda for the training program has been reported in detail elsewhere (Snyder, 1972). Data for the study were collected during the summer of 1971. The field teams made two site visits to each of the three facilities. During the first visit, physical data on the facility were collected and the administrator was interviewed. At this time, an observation schedule was mapped out for the next visits. During the second visit, which lasted for two days, field workers conducted observations and interviews. Site visits generally commenced around 9:30 in the morning and were terminated at about 4:00 in the afternoon. Each area where residents congregate was observed at least three times for approximately thirty minutes. The limitations of such short term observations as part of a cross-sectional study in contrast to longer observations and a longitudinal approach are recognized by both the author and the participants. The decision was made to carry out exploratory research at several facilities for comparative purposes rather than to concentrate on one facility in greater detail.

MAJOR FINDINGS

Clarification of Social Behavior: Implications for Future Researchers

Code specifications stipulate that "social areas" should be provided in a nursing home. It is expected that these social areas will promote social activities and conversations. Both researchers and practitioners are concerned that conversation occur among nursing home residents in order to promote physical and social rehabilitation (Lawton, 1968; Kramer, 1969; U.S. Congress, 1970: Lorenze, 1971). Based on our observations, designated social areas are not necessarily an inducement to conversation. If our goal is to develop opportunities and places for meaningful interpersonal exchanges between elderly residents, then three critical phases may be involved: bringing people together, having an appropriate physical and social setting for them to center around, and promoting conversation among these individuals. Clarification of these phases might serve to assist future researchers to direct investigations toward the dynamics of each phase in order to understand how to facilitate the desired behavior.

Three levels of social behavior appear most characteristic of aged nursing home residents: congregation, interaction, and conversation. By making distinctions among these three, it may be easier to identify the types of behavior exhibited, the relationship of each level to the physical and social setting, and the resultant effects of each level of social behavior. This conceptual scheme is an heuristic device; it is not intended to serve as a classification system.

Congregation

This refers to mere mutual presence in the same defined space or room. We observed several rooms where five to seven residents were seated for thirty minutes without appearing to acknowledge each other's presence. Staff members commented that residents sometimes stay in a lounge for hours without speaking to each other. *Impersonal interaction* is the term given to those instances where behavior of one person is stimulus to the behavior of another (English and English, 1958), but would not include a two-way verbal exchange of remarks. Impersonal interaction might include an instance where one man moves out of the way so a wheelchair may be pushed past him. *Conversation* involves an exchange of comments between two or more persons. In a nursing home, it might be necessary to distinguish between "social" and "individual" conversations. Social conversations involve the participation of two animate human beings; it is this type of conversation one attempts to promote for rehabilitation purposes. Individual conversations include those instances when people speak to themselves or to persons not visible to an outsider. Both of these types of conversation were observed in each of the nursing homes studied.

In sum, the focus should be on the user's needs and behavior, not on simply providing a lounge or a meeting place. By taking some of the preceding factors into account, the likelihood of creating a functionally social lounge increases greatly.

Content of Social Interaction

Much of the content of conversations involving the elderly nursing home residents seems to fall into two classes: routine and personal. Routine or ritualistic comments far outnumbered personal comments. This was particularly true of interactions between residents and staff members. Although many residents also engaged in routine conversations among themselves, residents occasionally conversed around more personally involving topics. For example, the residents sometimes explored each other's life styles or discussed the details of illnesses and rehabilitation progress. Notes on families and mutual community experiences were also shared.

There is some evidence that certain persons among the aged residents serve as "conversation catalysts." When these individuals are present, conversation and participation in spontaneous conversation increased.

Some external events that spark conversations were also tentatively identified. These include views from the window, arrivals and departures, odors (such as food or excrement), sounds, and unconventional resident behavior. Our data confirm Zinberg and Kaufman's evidence that a great deal of time is spent verbalizing about bodily functions (1963). This is particularly true in two of the three homes when absent staff members had to be called to move residents to rest rooms. None of the three facilities was designed with lavatory facilities close to lounges or dayrooms. Since staff members did not appear to visit dayrooms with any predictable regularity, residents often resorted to prolonged chanting to signal their needs. A meaningful research question would be to investigate whether some residents stay in their bedrooms in order to have easy access to essential and frequently used facilities. This would be one example of design and staffing patterns influencing the congregation patterns or social behavior of residents in a nursing home.

Settings of Social Behavior

Based on the writing of Sommer (1969) and Lawton (1970), we originally planned to study social behavior in dayrooms, lounges, and dining areas. We extended this scope and considered any area or room where groups of residents congregate, regardless of the designated title. Based on this function-oriented definition, social areas in these nursing homes included: dayrooms, floor lounges, dining rooms, hallways, some bedrooms, some activity rooms, and certain therapy rooms. Although residents did congregate in each of these places, not all provided a setting conducive to conversation. Vicarious social activity may lead to participatory activity; however, this is not always the case. The distinction appears to be important in terms of the relationship between the rehabilitation oriented facility, where over 50% of the residents participated in therapy classes or other activities, use of lounges was substantially lower.

The function of a lounge may be determined, then, by both existing alternatives and by the type of persons who are likely to utilize the area. From the point of view of the resident, it might be worthwhile to analyze both the range of persons one is likely to encounter each day, and the variety of physical spaces one is likely to occupy. In this way, some of the sterility of institutional life might be alleviated through positive steps to expand each resident's physical and social environment.

Activities and Social Interaction

Certain activities seem to be associated with social interaction while others appear to discourage it. We observed individuals making puzzles, knitting, arranging flowers, and reading newspapers or magazines. Each of these individual activities frequently served as a conversation prop by providing a focus of conversation (see Mehrabian and Diamond, 1971). Other persons, upon entering a room, would question the resident about some aspect of his activity. Looking out the window was another widely pursued activity in one of the nursing homes where the design permitted and facilitated it. This activity was pursued alone, in the presence of others, or jointly and accompanied by conversation. Even people classified as "confused" seemed capable of some participation in gazing out the windows.

Organized activities such as Reality Orientation, crafts, and eating did not necessarily spur conversations. For example, in activity rooms, conversation ebbs except when residents are completing a project or awaiting materials or instructions. Spontaneous conversation seems to distract from these activities. If, as we are told, the ability to concentrate is reduced in old age, then perhaps the person selects the most stimulating or relevant activity at that particular moment. Perhaps recreational therapists should pace an activity program with occasional conversation breaks. This might promote the formation of new social relationships as well as accommodate shorter attention spans.

Furniture, Furniture Arrangement, and Social Relations

One of the more important design considerations when working with a nursing home population is recognition of the high frequency of reliance on prosthetic walking devices. In the three nursing homes studied, about 85% of the residents require some prosthetic aid in order to be mobile. In most of the thirty-four observations made, over half of the residents were seated in wheelchairs. One particular type of wheelchair, the geriatric wheelchair, seems to impose certain constraints on the individual. The chair's small wheel diameter renders a resident immobile. Residents' comments indicate that persons seated in such chairs are assumed to be ill, incapacitated, or confused. Due to the disproportionately large chair size, persons seated in geriatric wheelchairs are frequently relegated to their own area in a lounge, dining, or activity room, and the chair's immobility keeps them there. The geriatric wheelchair creates a basis for behavior discrimination and personal segregation. Furthermore, the arbitrariness of this social imprisonment is tragic. Staff members in two of the three facilities stated that not all persons in such chairs actually need the support or restraint provided, but that it is often easier to transport and to monitor patients seated in the geriatric wheelchair.

The conventional nursing home frequently uses professional interior design or interior decoration assistance. Many decorators blithely assume that a room must have a certain "normal" or "homelike" appearance. This entails such trappings as sofas, chairs, and coffee tables—all closely arranged in conversational groups. There is little recognition that many residents are in the nursing home because they cannot walk and are confined to wheelchairs. Open spaces or voids serve as an unfulfilled challenge awaiting the decorator's talents of furniture selection. Residents in wheelchairs are virtually banished from these overdone spaces. Wheelchairs cannot be maneuvered easily and unusable chairs swallow up choice seating locations. In two of the three homes studied, fewer than a fifth of the chairs in any dayroom or lounge were observed in use. These unused chairs become obstacles and actually impede group formation rather than promote social interaction. A better solution might be to have a couple of easily moveable chairs and other accessible stacking chairs which visitors or staff members would use as necessary. Wide open spaces would allow free access to areas within the room and would alleviate the tendency for wheelchair-type to determine resident placement within a room.

From the money saved on chairs, the management might consider investing in a few more tables. Based on several observations, it seems clear that tables of a conventional height do have a unique and important function in the nursing home environment. As previously mentioned, the residents often like to watch out windows when they overlook "entertaining" sights such as highways, jails, parking lots, schools, farms, subway stations, or bird sanctuaries. The usual pattern of seating is to place chairs in one line at the window. But, by placing a table in front of the window and having the residents gather around it, several desireable things begin to happen. Tables enable residents to maintain their view from the window while affording the opportunity to establish eye contact with more people than the side-by-side seating allows. The table also seems to provide other beneficial psychological effects. The table top serves as a visual shield. Since many signs of infirmity (i.e., wheelchairs, catheter collection bags, leg problems) are hidden beneath the table, attention is focused on the more functional parts of the body. A table screens out the infirmities and allows old people to concentrate on each other as individuals. Making a few tables available and placing them in front of windows may be a fairly easy and subtle way of conversation and physical and social rehabilitation (Lawton, 1968). For example, although hallways or areas around nursing stations and elevators seem to be sites of congregation, conversations in these areas were limited to greetings and orientations. Constant arrivals, departures, and interruptions inhibited extended discussions most of the time. An alternative arrangement for providing visual stimulation and yet allowing for prolonged conversations was to gather in a dayroom in view of the nursing station or hallway. This seating location allowed people to watch from afar, yet to converse if the opportunity presented itself.

Conversation levels increased during the early morning and again prior to meal times in two of the facilities studied. Perhaps residents had more ideas, facts, and experiences to exchange during these times of the day. Conversations also seemed to be stimulated by the presence or absence of visitors. Often the visitors would become the focus of resident attention and other conversations between residents would dwindle as all eyes turned toward the newcomers. On the other hand, visitors sometimes promoted conversations when they drew others who were present into their group.

The notion we are left with is that designating a social area does not guarantee the promotion of either congregation, impersonal interaction, or social conversation. To examine further some of the events that seem to bring people together and to promote interaction and conversation, several other factors were studied.

Factors Influencing Congregation

When we examined the residents' use of dayrooms, lounges, dining rooms, therapy areas, and hallways, several principles emerged. It seems that residents may be located in an area (including a potential social area) for any one of at least three reasons:

1. A space may provide a source of certain services. At times, one may find that use or occupancy of a space is instrumental in meeting needs.
2. A space may have certain attributes which make it inherently appealing. A fascinating view from one window or a comfortable chair may draw individuals to one location over another when all else is equal.
3. An individual may occupy or be taken to a room or space by the staff for some administrative or program reasons. These objectives may not be known to the resident, but are perhaps known and determined by someone else who has control over him or over his actions.

These listed items point out two levels of behavior: motivation and control. In the first two items, the resident is motivated and is in control of his own actions. The third item obviates resident motivation and assumes that the resident has no control over his placement. These suggestions reflect the nature of the behavior observed in nursing homes and are probably not applicable to non-institutionalized individuals.

Patient segregation by mental or physical ability status is currently a controversial topic in social gerontology. Brody (1970) and Badar, et al. (1971) suggest that separating patients by mental ability is more efficient and less distressing for the more able elderly residents. Kahana and Kahana (1970; Kahana, 1971) have found that aged patients benefit from interaction with less able as well as more able individuals. In the present study, we found that the mode of patient segregation (whether it be on the basis of sex, mobility level, or mental status) often determined both patterns of room use and of room activity.

For example, in one facility, there were three nursing units housing patients of three ability levels: mentally alert and able to be independently mobile and/or self-propelling, requiring intermediate supervision due to mental and/or physical disorders, bedridden and/or senile. The residents of the most able nursing unit had only one lounge. In this lounge, men and women congregated at will; there were generally several clutches of residents talking, playing cards, or making puzzles. In three other lounges, we did not see one male resident or staff member. Female staff members were often required to wheel patients to the lounges. Staff members habitually lined residents up along the windows in a single row. Few residents were engaged in any activities other than watching out the window or talking to a person to one side of them. These residents were generally exposed only to other women like themselves; use of a lounge was determined by the location of one's bedroom on the ward.

In another nursing home, where three lounges were available to the residents, a tiny lobby was often packed with residents. Six to eight persons, who would wheel their own chairs or walk by themselves, drew together before and/or after meals and watched others or talked. In the same nursing home, another lounge was populated by persons in geriatric wheelchairs and by day patients. There was no television, no unsheathed window, and only limited conversation. This lounge seemed to attract less physically and less mentally adept residents. Even though the facility itself was not rigorously segregated by ability type, the lounges and areas within these lounges did have concentrations of similarly able or disabled residents.

In the third facility, where an extensive rehabilitation program was offered, small solaria on each nursing unit were used by the less able residents who did not regularly participate in recreation, occupational or physical therapy. The larger facility-wide lounges were used by persons of virtually every status during the late afternoon when visitors are present in these areas. We found several other indications that activity programs influence the demand for social areas, and hence the tendency for persons of certain ability levels to congregate. In two of the nursing homes, where organized activities were run for small proportions (10%) of the residents, lounges were used continually throughout the day. At promoting acquaintance. This does not mean that an unalterable design principle has been arrived at, and that all window space should be treated in this manner. The table, as Sommer (1969) observed, also provides a working surface for either individual or shared activities, especially when such items as books, magazines and newspapers, puzzles, and/or sewing projects are stored nearby on accessible shelves.

CONCLUSIONS

The success of an exploratory study may be judged in terms of the questions or ideas it raises rather than by its proscriptions for change. Analysis of the social, physical, and organizational structure of three nursing homes has raised the following issues. Each invites further research.

1. It may be worthwhile to look at social behavior in terms of three phases (congregation, impersonal interaction, and conversation) in order to understand how each facilitates or hinders other desireable behavior.
2. The title of a room or designation of an area may have little bearing on the function of that space. Social behavior is not confined to dayrooms or lounges. Dayroom and lounge existence does not guarantee congregation, impersonal interaction, or conversation.
3. Socially designated spaces may be unused as settings of social behavior for several reasons:
    a. Due to immobility, residents are unable to either get to the dayroom or to make adequate use of the resources of this room.
    b. Since services such as restrooms and nursing stations are generally distantly placed from most lounges, residents may prefer to stay in their bedrooms or meet in halls. Bedrooms and hallway locations place the individual in a position where summoning aid or meeting one's own needs is facilitated.
    c. The lounge provides no more interesting or entertaining stimuli than some other area such as the recreation room, hallway, or bedroom.
4. Various forms of patient segregation, whether externally imposed by nursing unit regulations or by activity scheduling, or individually imposed due to greater freedom of the more able residents to move, may severely limit the physical and social environment of many institutionalized elderly. By analyzing each individual's physical and social environment, one might be in a better position to make changes which would enrich the individual's daily life.
5. Interior designers and decorators must be attuned to the particular physical characteristics and needs of aging nursing home residents so that their efforts reinforce the overall goals of the facility.

6. Specific items of furniture may have a profound effect on social behavior.
   a. Tables may focus attention on the more functional parts of the aged person's body, increase eye contact, and create a surface for other focal activities. Tables may induce all phases of social behavior: congregation, impersonal interaction, and conversation.
   b. Geriatric wheelchairs may become a resident's total environment and cause him to be both physically and socially alienated from either congregation or conversation with other residents.
7. If conversation is one means of reinforcing physical and social rehabilitation of the elderly, then perhaps codes should be directed toward more than mere provision of dayrooms of a certain size. Guidelines for promoting meaningful social encounters between the elderly and between elderly and staff members might be most helpful to nursing home administrators.

ACKNOWLEDGMENT

The author gratefully acknowledges the conceptual advice and editorial assistance of Dr. Edward R. Ostrander.

REFERENCES

American Nursing Home Association. *Nursing home fact book 1970-1971.* Washington, D.C.: ANHA Publication 107, 1971.

Anderson, Nancy N. Institutionalization, interaction, and self-conception in aging. In: A. M. Rose and W. A. Peterson (Eds.), *Older people and their social world.* Philadelphia: F. A. Davis, 1965.

Badar, J. E., Maxwell, W. H., and Watson, W. I. Restrictions on movement in a home for the aged. Paper presented at the 24th Annual Meeting of the Gerontological Society, Houston, Texas, November, 1971.

Bergman, M. Changes in hearing with age. *Gerontologist*, 1971, 11, 148-151.

Barker, R. G. and Barker, Louise S. The psychological ecology of old people in midwest, Kansas, and Yoredale, Yorkshire. *Journal of gerontology*, 1961, 16, 144-149.

Bell, T. The relationship between social involvement and feeling old among residents in homes for the aged. *Journal of gerontology*, 1967, 22, 17-22.

Bennett, Ruth G. Distinguishing characteristics of the aging from a sociological viewpoint. *Journal of the American geriatrics society*, 1968, 16, 127-135.

Brody, Elaine M. Congregate care facilities and mental health of the elderly. *Aging and human development*, 1970, 1, 279-321.

Carp, Frances M. The impact of the environment on old people. *Gerontologist*, 1967, 7, 106-108.

Cumming, M. Elaine. New thought on the theory of disengagement. In: R. Kastenbaum (Ed.), *New thoughts on old age.* New York: Springer, 1964, 3-18.

Cumming, M. Elaine and Henry, W. E. *Growing old: the process of disengagement.* New York: Basic Books, 1961.

DeLong, A. J. The micro-spatial structure of the older person: some implications of planning the social and spatial environment. In: L. A. Pastalan and D. H. Carson (Eds.), *Spatial behavior of older people*. Ann Arbor: Univ. of Mich., 1970, 68-87.

Derrick, W. P. and Kagan, M. Social behavior of state hospital nursing home patients. *Gerontologist*, 1967, 7, 283-285.

Donahue, Wilma. Impact of living arrangements on ego development in the elderly. In: F. M. Carp and W. M. Burnett (Eds.), *Patterns of living and housing middle-aged and older people*. Public Health Service Publication, No. 1496. Washington, D. C.: U.S. Dept. HEW, 1966.

English, H. G. and English, A. C. *A comprehensive dictionary of psychological and psychoanalytical terms*. New York: Longmans, Green, 1958, 270.

Freese, A. S. Dr. René Dubos speaks. *Modern maturity*, 1971, 14 (4), 58-60.

Goffman, E. *Asylums*. Garden City, New York: Doubleday, 1961.

Ittelson, W. H. Environmental psychology of the psychiatric ward. In: C. W. Taylor, R. Bailey, and C. H. Hardin-Branch (Eds.), *Second national conference on architectural psychology*, May 26-28, 1966. Salt Lake City: University of Utah, 1967, Section 3, 1-12.

Ittelson, W. H., Rivlin, Leanne G., Proshansky, H. M. The use of behavioral maps in environmental psychology. In: H. M. Proshansky, W. H. Ittelson, and L. G. Rivlin (Eds.), *Environmental psychology–man and his physical setting*. New York: Holt, 1970, 419-439.

Kahana, B. and Kahana Eva. Changes in mental status of elderly patients in age-integrated and age-segregated hospital milieus. *Journal of abnormal psychology*, 1970, 75, 177-181.

Kahana, Eva. Emerging issues in institutional services for the aging. *Gerontologist*, 1971, 11, 51-58.

Kramer, C. H. What's needed to get patients outside their dependent selves: effective communication. *Modern nursing home*, 1969, 23 (3), 71-73.

Lawton, M. P. Ecology and aging. In: L. A. Pastalan and D. H. Carson (Eds.), *Spatial behavior of older people*. Ann Arbor: Univ. of Mich. Press, 1970, 40-67.

Lawton, M. P. Social rehabilitation of the aged. *Journal of the American geriatrics society*, 1968, 16, 1346-1363.

Lawton, M. P. The human being and the institutional building. In: C. Burnett, J. Lang, and D. Vaschon (Eds.), *Architecture for human behavior: collected papers from a human behavior mini conference and exhibit, Nov. 11, 1971*. Philadelphia: Philadelphia Chapter American Institute of Architects, 1971, 31-40.

Lawton, M. P., Liebowitz, B., and Charon, H. Physical structure and the behavior of senile patients following ward remodeling. *Aging and human development*, 1970, 1, 231-239.

Lipman, A. Old people's homes: siting and neighbourhood integration. *Sociological review*, 1967, 15, 323-338.

Lorenze, E. J. Extended Care. *Journal of the American geriatrics society*, 1971, 19, 417-422.

Mason, Evelyn. Some correlates of self-judgments of the aged. *Journal of gerontology*, 1954, 9, 324-337.

Mehrabian, A. and Diamond, Shirley G. Effects of furniture arrangement, props, and personality on social interaction. *Journal of personality and social psychology*, 1971, 20, 18-30.

Messer, M. The possibility of an age-concentrated environment becoming a normative system. *Gerontologist*, 1967, 7, 247-251.

Rosow, I. Housing and local ties of the aged. *Patterns of living and housing of middle-aged and older people: Proceedings of research conference*, Washington, D.C.: U.S. Dept. HEW, 1965, 47-57.

Scott, Frances G. Factors in the personal adjustment of institutionalized and non-institutionalized aged. *American sociological review*, 1955, 20, 538-546.

Sommer, R. *Personal space*. Englewood Cliffs, N.J.: Prentice Hall, 1969.

Sommer, R. Small group ecology in institutions for the elderly. In: L. A. Pastalan and D. H. Carson (Eds.), *Spatial behavior of older people*. Ann Arbor: Univ. of Mich. Press, 1970, 25-39.

Snyder, Lorraine H. Patterns of social interaction, organization, and facility design in three nursing homes–An exploratory investigation. Unpublished Master of Arts Thesis, Cornell University, Ithaca, N.Y., 1972.

Stotsky, B. A. *The nursing home and the aged psychiatric patient*. New York: Appleton, Century, Crofts, 1970.

Tec, Nechama & Granick, Ruth. Social isolation and difficulties in social interaction of residents of a home for aged. *Social problems*, 1959-1960, 8, 226-232.

Tissue, T. and Wells, L. Antecedent life styles and old age. *Psychological reports*, 1971, 29, 1100.

U. S. Congress. Senate. U. S. Senate Committee on Finance, Special Committee on Aging, Summary of Medicare and Medicaid problems, issues, and alternatives. *Developments in aging, 1969*, Washington, D.C.: U.S. Government, 1970, 91-875.

U. S. Dept. HEW. Social Security Administration, HIM-3, Federal Health Insurance for the Aged. *Conditions of participation; extended care facilities*. Code of Federal Regulations, Title 20, Chapter III, part 405, March, 1966.

Wax, M. Changing role of homes for the aged. *Gerontologist*, 1962, 2, 128-133.

Zinberg, N. E. and Kaufman, I. Cultural and personality factors associated with aging: an introduction. In: N. E. Zinberg & I. Kaufman (Eds.), *Normal psychology of the aging process*. New York: International Universities Press, 1963, 17-71.

chapter 7

RESEARCH BASED NURSING HOME DESIGN: AN APPROACH FOR PLANNING ENVIRONMENTS FOR THE AGING[1]

Edward R. Ostrander, Ph.D.

> In review one becomes doubly aware of how scant the hard evidence is (on designing for aged with disabilities). It is hoped, however, that the many assertions and armchair arguments may lead some who have the chance to observe structures in use to check them out empirically.
>
> M. Powell Lawton (1971, pp. 39-40)

It was the objective of this research "to observe structures in use" employing a variety of methods in order to gather empirical data that might increase our understanding of the impact of environmental settings and social mechanics on the behavior of institutionalized aged people.

This paper presents our orientation regarding man-environment relations, our frame of reference for studying this relationship and the research strategy employed in empirical investigation of six extended care facilities in New York State.

[1] This paper was funded by Hatch 407 from the New York State Agriculture Experiment Station at Cornell University as part of the Gerontology Project: Research in Environmental Analysis and Design for the Aging.

PHYSICAL SETTING AND SOCIAL MECHANICS AS INFLUENCES ON BEHAVIOR

Before considering the specific questions dealt with in this research on the relationship between the physical environment and the behavior of aged persons, it is essential to confront a broader and more basic question. Is there a relationship between the physical environment and the behavior and attitudes of human beings? There are practitioners who will argue that the physical environment is totally insignificant as a behavioral influence. They would contend that administrative policies, the social tone set by the facility staff and management, relations between people, and individual psychological quirks are *really* what count in shaping human behavior. People with different professional training and experience are equally willing to declare that influences on behavior resulting from the physical setting are of major importance while social and interpersonal factors recede into irrelevance. Lawton (1968, 1969), Friedman and Coleman (1970), Miller (1968) consider these issues.

Our stance is more moderate and closer to the middle of the continuum. We agree with Mayer Spivack (1971, p. 3), Director of the Department of Environmental Analysis and Design in the Laboratory of Community Psychiatry at the Harvard Medical School, when he hypothesizes:

> . . . under many circumstances the environment recedes into the background, but that there are occasions when the intensity of environmental imputs or arrangement of circumstances intrudes upon the person to inhibit or cause a malfunction or annoyance of the ongoing behavior.

What a physical setting will do to behavior of the people using that space is not simply a result of the number of square feet available to each person, the floor plan, or the color of the wall. The person is being acted upon by a complex of variables or factors that are both physical and social. His situation at any given moment involves a field of forces operating in dynamic fashion, not a static condition. To ignore some factors that are either physical or social and to isolate others for special attention may guarantee misunderstanding of the environment-behavior relationship.

Our position is not that the physical environment is all important, nor that it is of no importance. There are subtle but extremely important interactions occurring between the physical setting in which behavior takes place, the prevailing social norms and expectations, and the social participants generating and responding to stimulation.

INSTITUTIONAL OBJECTIVES, HUMAN BEHAVIOR, AND PHYSICAL STRUCTURE

Raymond Studer (1967, 1969), an architect well grounded in psychological writing, provides a frame of reference for considering the man-environment relationship that lends itself to the study of institutional facilities. He contends we must understand the institution's goals, the behaviors needed for goal achievement, and whether the physical setting facilitates or inhibits those goal directed behaviors.

An extended care facility is established to enable people to convalesce in a supportive environment in order to regain their physical and mental health and self reliance (Freeman, 1971). There are appropriate behaviors that the people who use the facilities should engage in as a means of achieving the goals for which the institution was created. In an extended care facility, patient mobility and social interaction are desirable behaviors. If we find that the physical layout discourages the behaviors essential for goal achievement, we have an institutional structure that is, to some degree, non-functional.

Studer further claims that a building is never really frozen into a final form. He sees it as a living experiment that must be designed, studied, and redesigned to meet the changing needs of the users. If needs change or improved ways to achieve the goals are uncovered, building alterations may be essential.

AN APPROACH: ENVIRONMENTAL ANALYSIS

In line with Studer's recommendation that goals must be the starting point, it is necessary to understand the facility's charter and management's view of the mission. Based on our research we were able to identify several additional essential concerns: the desires of various groups of users, the range of activities and behaviors of the users, and the context or setting in which these occur.

To marshall this information, an orderly procedure called "environmental analysis" can be employed. I define environmental analysis as *the systematic study of the physical and social arrangements within which behavior occurs and needs are satisfied*.

The environmental analyst subscribes to a social science orientation and seeks to find answers to six fundamental questions.

The questions are:

1. What objectives or goals are these physical facilities and social arrangements created to accomplish?

   The mental hospital facility is created to rehabilitate the mentally ill. The home for the aged exists to make the later years of one's life physically and socially comfortable, challenging, and meaningful.
2. Is there a particular philosophy or theory to be followed to achieve these objectives?

   There is a theory or at least an operating philosophy that should lead to the achievement of the goals. Assumptions are made regarding the most effective way to achieve rehabilitation objectives. Medical and physiological principles as well as rehabilitation theory provide the foundation for the activity programs and physical arrangements in the extended care facility.

3. What behaviors or activities must be carried out?

   To achieve the objectives and operate within the theory or philosophy, various groups of users must accomplish certain tasks or acts. For example, residents require specific services, staff members deliver some of these services, and residents must carry out designated behaviors before the rehabilitation cycle will occur. Many of these essential behaviors can be identified by specific staff members involved.

4. Where do these behaviors and activities happen?

   A detailed description of the physical arrangements wherein the activities take place is essential information. For example, in what extended care facility spaces do physical activities take place and where does meaningful social interaction occur?

5. What kinds of staff skills, procedures, and programs have been developed and put into practice to help achieve the objectives?

   The number of staff members and their talents are critical considerations for the smooth operation of any service delivery system. For instance, in the case of mental and physical rehabilitation, arts and crafts or physiotherapy may bring patients and staff together in an informal way. This interaction may encourage the residents in their rehabilitation efforts and also provide stimulating activity.

6. When and in what sequence are goal-related behaviors exhibited by staff and by residents?

   Observation of behaviors in any setting reveals interesting patterns over time. Some spaces in institutional settings are more fully occupied during certain hours of the day than during other hours. Study of the use of the facilities over the course of the day suggest more efficient design or use of space.

ENVIRONMENTAL DESIGN BASED ON ENVIRONMENTAL ANALYSIS

There is considerable merit to the contention that environmental design cannot occur without environmental analysis. Larsen (1967) discusses the relationship of research on behavior as a prelude to environmental design. Sanoff and Cohen (1969) declare that the environmental designer's task is to understand the environment, and to create effective new environmental systems to meet man's needs. (These authors describe the environment as a complex adaptive or internally as well as externally open system.) Analyzing and solving environmental problems dictates multi-disciplinary collaboration since any discipline by its very nature focuses on a segment of the environment or behavior.

The *EDRA I* (Sanoff and Cohen, 1969, p. V) preface clarifies these ideas further by noting that:

> The basic types of explorations which form the core of environmental design are: the externalization of the pertinent design process in the construction of models of these processes; the application of systematic and system's approaches to the design process; and [the development of social and behavioral knowledge as to the man-environmental relationship].

The environmental analyst's mission is to assemble empirical information about users or potential users of facilities to provide a basis for improving the ways these facilities function. The users of any facility are not just the residents but also visitors, the staff, and the management.

THE RESEARCHER'S APPROACH TO DATA GATHERING

Barker (1965) has noted a distinction in the researcher's function in data gathering that he believes dramatically alters the nature of the data. He contends that psychologists may function as "transducers" who merely serve as recording devices when they observe behavior. In contrast, they may also function as "operators" manipulating the situation, the people in the situation, and to a considerable extent predetermining the nature of the behavioral output the participants will reveal. Barker claims that the type of data generated when the researcher carries out these two distinct roles reveals a very different picture of human behavior. He is concerned that we not assume the "real" picture of human behavior is the one revealed when the psychologist functions as an operator.

In a similar vein, David Canter (1970) makes the distinction between users of facilities being studied as "subjects" and as "objects." When a user is seen as an "object," the emphasis is on the observation of their overt behavior and does not involve personal interaction with the user. In contrast, the user seen as the "subject" is conversed with, asked to respond subjectively, and to offer his own personal interpretations of the situation.

The researchers concluded that the optimum procedure is one that incorporates both approaches. Ostrander (1972) has translated the Barker and Canter distinctions into terms of research instruments and data gathering procedures. He arrays these procedures along a continuum ranging from obtrusive intervening techniques to unobtrusive nonintervening techniques. The pool of techniques must be developed for use with both research orientations described by Barker and Canter. At the present time the number of well-developed techniques is limited.

THE ENVIRONMENTAL ASSESSMENT BATTERY

By collecting diverse information about the users and the physical setting employing techniques created to tap different facets of the user-environment relationship, we have an approach that parallels the concept of the personality test battery. The object in using a personality test battery is to get a comprehensive picture of the personality. This picture would include information on intelligence, motivation, predispositions, attitudes, interests, and abilities. The quantitative configuration that the battery provides is consistent with the definition of personality as the unique organization or relatively enduring psychological characteristics possessed by an individual, as revealed by his interaction with the environment (McKeachie and Doyle 1966, p. 410). A graphic representation of the results of a personality test battery, called a psycho-graph, shows the standing of the individual in relation to a group norm in a simple-to-understand visual form. The advantage of the battery over a single measuring instrument is the comprehensiveness of the information provided.

The use of an environmental assessment battery is based on the same reasoning. By using a number of approaches, we can understand the setting and learn how users behave and feel about their environment so a more complete picture is available. In contrast, if only one technique were employed, we would be provided with only a limited amount of information.

In our study of extended care facilities we have made exploratory use of the multi-dimensional approach and collected data using both unobtrusive as well as obtrusive techniques. Systematic observations were made of activities in the setting and interviews were carried out with administrators, staff, and patients. Photographic evidence was also collected and incidental observations were recorded.

THE ASSESSMENT BATTERY, CONSTRUCT VALIDITY, AND DATA CREDIBILITY

By accumulating a diverse array of information it may be possible to pursue a construct validity approach in arriving at conclusions about the meaning of the information collected. Construct validity of any measurement techniques refers to the degree to which it, in fact, provides an appropriate basis for making inferences regarding the construct it purports to measure (Kelly 1969, p. 48). The environmental assessment approach used here involves observations and qualitative data. The precise measurement of variables by any one instrument is not the issue. The validity of the inferences is our concern. Information from the observations and other open-ended techniques generally do not provide precise quantitative data.

For example, if the inference is made that a particular physical feature such as a steep ramp constitutes an architectural barrier, it may be possible to demonstrate that fact by drawing on interview data from residents and conversations with staff and management. If the systematic observation data and photographic evidence offers additional support for a specific interpretation, then the weight of evidence begins to remove the conclusion from the realm of subjective judgment that might be the case if there was but one source of data.

The body of empirical information pertaining to human behavior and the built environment is limited, and many empirical findings are preliminary or tentative. The limited work available also means that the instruments or techniques are relatively untested. Given this state of the art, a healthy tradition has begun to develop among some workers in the environmental design area and it bodes well for the sound development of design decisions based on systematic and rational procedures. The tradition consists of working out a credibility rating system or an evaluative judgment of the supporting evidence that is being used as a basis for suggesting courses of action and for the development of design hypotheses.

Two illustrative credibility rating systems will be described briefly. Mayer Spivack (1971) used a rating form that had three major credibility categories or levels with subdivisions. The highest credibility was:

Rating I: Systematic research strongly supports finding X

Rating II: Unsystematic and/or qualitative research to support testable hypotheses

Rating III: Speculation or informal observation—may or may not be testable.

When the researcher draws conclusions or makes recommendations, he gives the credibility rating of the evidence on which he bases them. This permits the designers or other decision makers to determine for themselves in light of the evidence cited whether they agree with the position taken.

Sanoff (1969), in a discussion of systematic approaches to design, points out the problems of making accurate predictions of future events from a limited set of past observations. He lists six bases for "making reasonable guesses about the future behavior of the system to be designed" (1969, p. 5). These include drawing on similar prior cases, analogue prediction, or extrapolation from corresponding events. Other procedures are experimentation, black-box simulation or mock ups, introspective prediction rooted in experience, and the most daring: taking the risk in a totally unpredictable situation.

In this research project we are working in that cautious tradition of making guarded pronouncements when the evidence is sketchy. This is not an experiment which might be expected to produce data of maximum predictability. An experiment was not possible because the issues we were interested in could only be pursued *in situ*. It is our conviction that the institutional setting could not be replicated in the laboratory. It can only be understood if it is studied as it actually exists.

We have not developed a credibility rating system for interpreting our work. Instead we are using an approach that attempts to make self evident the significance of what is happening in the institutional setting. It is our belief that changes made in the physical arrangements or social mechanisms in extended care facilities will come about through the increased sensitivity of the administrators and staff, designers, and interested professional organizations. Authoritative dictates from researchers and other people far removed from the institutional setting and its daily functioning may be inappropriate at this time.

It is possible to provide significant information in comprehendable form by employing a multi-dimensional data gathering approach and by working with techniques that involve considerable visual evidence in the form of photographs and observational technique graphics. These are supplemented by the social scientist's traditional tool, the interview.

Our approach is closer to that used by the anthropologist when visiting another culture. He does not barge in and impose himself upon the lives and culture of the people he seeks to understand. Instead, he tries to be an unobtrusive observer of events. Hopefully, he becomes a participant observer whose presence is acknowledged, but with the passage of time, less recognized. There is evidence from the behavior and comments of the residents and staff studied that field workers during the research team's one to two day's stay tended to become "part of the furnishings." The amount of resident or staff behavior that could be classified as "playing-to-the-researchers" appeared to be minimal.

OPTIONS AND LIMITATIONS IN FACILITY DESIGN DECISION-MAKING

When planning an extended care facility, decision-makers and architects operate under a number of restraints. For example, codes stipulate certain quantitative requirements related to space allocation and location. Budgetary considerations set limits on virtually every aspect of planning. Frequently officers of the state agencies who approve of construction loans and/or mortgages set up criteria that must be met in planning and design. Local ordinances and unions also determine certain aspects of construction. All of these factors must be accommodated to throughout the decision-making or programming phases of facility design. An environmental analyst should be familiar with the form of these constraints as one important aspect of his data gathering.

ENVIRONMENTAL ANALYSIS CONTRASTED WITH EVALUATION

In considering these man-environment functionality issues it is important to make a distinction between inspection or evaluation and environmental analysis. In an inspection of a facility, the goal is to determine the presence or absence of building features covered by code specifications that pertain to safety and building functionality as a physical system (i.e., plumbing, heating, etc.) In the minds of many laymen the idea of inspection or evaluation has a negative connotation.

The thrust of evaluation is seen by many as one of identifying problems and chastising those responsible in the manner of the Nader consumer group (Townsend, 1971) or a governmental commission.

In contrast to the negative tone of inspection or evaluation, environmental analysis looks at an institutional facility in terms of its goals, the functions that are performed within it, and the behavior engaged in by occupants. Environmental analysis connotes a problem solving orientation. In a setting occupied by aged people with physical disabilities or sensory inadequacies, certain unique needs have to be met. These are inevitable because of the nature of the service provided and the population served. In that sense we could consider many of these to be almost universal issues because they are encountered in the majority of the facilities. In addition we also find some issues that are unique to a given facility.

By discussing these issues with staff and administration, as well as visiting facilities and observing behavior, we discover valid innovative solutions to the common problems.

There are three opportunities for using this information in alleviating problems.

1. When planning to build an addition to a facility or start a new facility. If the decision makers can become acquainted with solutions others have found successful or suggestions for potentially worthwhile solutions, they are likely to be more effective in spending their construction money.
2. When major renovations are being anticipated.
3. By using the evidence from environmental analysis for reviewing and revising regular maintenance activity and the daily operation of the facility.

The environmental analyst who studies nursing homes and extended care facilities gains an overview and is in a position to:

1. gather empirical data pertaining to problems of man and his environment

2. generate suggestions for new solutions and share them with those individuals responsible for providing these services
3. record solutions that have proven feasible in pragmatic situations
4. perform a clearing-house function for information pertaining to these problems.

Though the techniques used by the environmental analyst will provide data that will permit evaluation, the total orientation is different. We are seeking to find prototypical solutions in any setting that might be generalizable to other comparable institutional settings.

Although we have been talking primarily about architectural structure, built objects, and human behavior, the vital role of the social mechanisms in delivering the necessary services should not be overlooked. Training users, including administrators and staff, to maximally employ the potential of their physical setting is a critical, though often neglected, consideration.

We have tried to develop a philosophy for working with service delivery systems, to devise techniques and procedures for gathering empirical data, and to find appropriate ways of understanding what the data have to say. An equally vital task has been to translate the findings into forms that are comprehensible to practitioners. Though they do not have extensive research training, they are the ones who can put research rooted recommendations into practice for the benefit of their residents and staff.

REFERENCES

Barker, R. Explorations in ecological psychology. *American Psychologist*, 1965, 20(1), 1-14.

Canter, D. Should we treat building users as subjects or objects? In D. Canter (Ed.), *Architectural psychology*. London: RIBA Publications, 1970, pp. 11-18.

Freeman, J. Post hospital care of the patient past 65. *Geriatrics*, 1971, 26(5), 121-128.

Friedman, S. L., and Coleman, Mary Ann. Evaluation of medical facilities in institutions for the aged. In Minna Field (Ed.), *Depth and extent of the geriatric problem*. Springfield, Illinois: Charles Thomas, 1970, pp. 213-231.

Kelly, E. L. *Assessment of human characteristics*. Belmont, California: Books/Cole, 1969.

Larson, T. Research as a prelude to environmental design. In C. Taylor, R. Bailey and C. H. Branch (Eds.), *Second national conference on architectural psychology*. Salt Lake City: University of Utah, 1967, pp. 12:1-12:15.

Lawton, M. P. Social rehabilitation of the aged. *Journal of the American Geriatrics Society*, 1968, 16(12), 1346-1363.

Lawton, M. P. The human being and the institutional building. In C. Burnette, et al. (Eds.), *Architecture for human behavior*. Philadelphia: The American Institute for Architects, 1971, pp. 31-40.

McKeachie, W. and Doyle, C. *Psychology*. Reading, Massachusetts: Addison-Wesley, 1966.

Miller, M. The extended care facility: A commentary on definition. *Journal of the American Geriatric Society*. 1968, 16(7), 1012-1029.

Ostrander, E. The environmental analyst's tool kit: Options and cautions. Unpublished manuscript, New York State College of Human Ecology, Cornell University, Ithaca, New York, April, 1972.

Sanoff, H. A systematic approach to design. Unpublished mimeographed report, Design Research Laboratory Working Paper, School of Design, North Carolina State University, Raleigh, North Carolina, April, 1969.

Sanoff, H. and S. Cohn (Eds.), EDRA I: Proceedings of the 1st annual Environmental Design Research Association Conference. Raleigh, North Carolina, 1970.

Spivack, M. A place to eat, research report series: Number one. Unpublished mimeographed report, Laboratory of Community Psychiatry, Harvard Medical School, Boston, Massachusetts, 1971.

Studer, R. Some aspects of the man-designed environment interface. In G. Coates, and K. Moffett, (Eds.), *Response to the environment*. Raleigh, North Carolina: North Carolina State University, 1969, pp. 77-98.

Studer, R. The dynamics of behavior-contingent physical systems. In *Proceedings of the Portsmouth Symposium on Design*. Portsmouth, England, December, 1967. In E. Proshansky, et al. (Eds.), *Environmental psychology*. New York: Holt, Rinehart and Winston, 1971, pp. 56-76.

Townsend, C. *Old age: The last segregation*. New York: Grossman, 1971.

chapter 8

EFFECTS OF THE LIVING ENVIRONMENT ON ACTIVITY AND USE OF TIME*

Frances M. Carp, Ph.D.

This is a report of the effects of expanded opportunities upon activity among elderly people. This paper is limited to activities as such. There is special question regarding old people's aptitude for making new friends and acquaintances [1]. Therefore activity scores having to do with interpersonal relationships and social behaviors are reported separately [2]. One basic issue is the extent to which activity rate depends upon intrapersonal vs. situational factors in old age: *can* provision of a different living environment change patterns of activity? In this instance, does moving to a living environment with more opportunity for activity increase activity? A second issue addresses the desirability of environmental manipulation of activity rate: if it is possible, *should* such intervention to undertaken? Enrichment of available activities may

*Data collection supported by a research grant from the Hogg Foundation for Mental Health, the University of Texas and by research grant # RO1 HD03653 from the National Institute for Child Health and Human Development; eight-year interval data processing and reporting supported by research grant # 93-P-57511/9 from the Administration on Aging.

comprise opportunity to meet previously frustrated needs or stress from excessive external pressure.

Theoretical Model

THE ORIGINAL MODEL FOR THE STUDY

The activity study is part of a broader longitudinal study begun in 1959-60. The general model for the study was designed in the Lewinian tradition, viewing behavior as some function of person in interaction with environment: B = f (P, E) [3]. A basic postulate was that, even in old age, environmental intervention can affect behavior. The study design was also in the tradition of Murray, positing the central role of need satisfaction in determining outcomes of the person-environment transaction [4]. A second basic postulate was that the living environments of elderly, poor applicants for public housing failed to meet their basic physical and psychological needs. The central hypothesis was that provision of a living environment with more appropriate need-satisfaction potentials would affect behavior by improving quality of adaptation and sense of well-being.

Since the study was initiated, considerable progress has been made in gerontological theory development, much of it following the concepts of Lewin and Murray. Pervin seems to express the general current opinion that these are the two theories of personality which give greatest attention to the issue of person-environment interaction, and therefore hold most promise for developing explanatory models [5].

THE MODEL OF LAWTON AND ASSOCIATES

The "ecological change model" is of particular interest and was given careful consideration [6-10]. However, it seems inapplicable to present purposes for four reasons, each stemming from a limitation on the model which was explicitly imposed or recognized by its designers:

1. its purpose is to understand pathology, it is concerned only with
2. aspects of the environment which can be described in terms of "demand quality,"
3. capacities of persons to respond to those demands, and
4. aspects of human response that can be viewed in evaluative terms.

Purpose: Understanding pathology—While Lawton and associates use content from gerontology to demonstrate their theoretical structure, they "suggest that the constructs are more generally applicable to any area involving the understanding of mental or social pathology." [8, 10] By implication, the gerontological application relates to pathology. The people in the present study, though elderly, were "normal." They were community residents, coping rather well with difficult living situations, and had been screened as capable of future independent living when first seen. Furthermore, the new environment was designed to improve life for the relatively intact elderly, and its tenants were expected to adapt positively in it.

View of the environment in terms only of demand qualities—In regard to environmental variables, the Lawton *et al.* model is explicitly limited to "demand quality," an abstraction, its authors recognize, "that represents only one of many ways of dimensionalizing the environment." [10] There is need to design environments which will not make excessive demands upon the old person, but it is also appropriate and necessary to consider the capacity of the environment to meet his needs. One major goal of the new living environment under investigation was to meet the activity needs of its tenants. The physical construction of the facility and the philosophy of its staff were activity oriented [11, 12].

Definition of the person in terms of capacities—Lawton's selection of relevant person traits is exclusively in terms of "competence" to meet environmental demands: "the theoretical upper limit of capacity in biological health, sensation-perception, motor behavior, and cognition." [7] However, the person-environment transaction is a mutual one: "The importance of the external world is both as a source of disturbance with which the individual must cope and as a source of supplies by means of which the organism fulfills its destiny. That is, the environment intrudes upon the organism .... while on the other hand the organism searches in the environment for what it needs." [13] "The organism cannot properly be compared to a keyboard on which external stimuli would play." [14]

> Environmental psychology is not a theory of determinism. It sees man not as a passive product of his environment, but as a goal-directed being who acts upon his environment and who in turn is influenced by it [15].

The participants of the present study were independently living members of the community who were taking self-initated action to meet their own needs. Every respondent had been carefully screened by the local Housing Authority staff and declared capable of independent living and, more specifically, capable of adjusting to the new environment and likely to benefit from it and to contribute to it. In attempting to use the Lawton model with such respondents, the restricted range on capacity variables may limit their ability to account for variance in outcomes of person-environment transaction. Besides, one may question whether capacities are the only or the most important person attributes in this context of evaluating the impact of living environments upon activities of the normal old. The study requires a model which includes the relevance of environmental resources to human needs as well as that of human capacities to environmental demands.

Evaluative view of behavior–The model of Lawton and associates considers "a limited aspect of human behavior," that which "can be viewed in evaluative terms." [10] In general the broader study is evaluative in considering desirable outcomes of person-environment transactions to be adaptive behavior and the experience of satisfaction. However, evaluative treatment of rates and types of activity would involve value judgements which are unwarranted in view of the prolonged and as yet unresolved controversy over the two approaches which have come to be known as the activity and disengagement theories of aging. In this sub-study, then, the model of Lawton *et al.* is inappropriate.

THE MODEL FOR THE PRESENT STUDY

Therefore the original model has been retained. Its main lines in relation to the activity analysis follow.

The role of capacities–Despite the importance of capacities within that segment of the population liable to pathological behavior as the outcome of the P-E transaction, it may be that–within the normal range of persons and environments–effects of basic capacities are minimal. The slopes of the lines or the shapes of the curves representing the relationships between P capacities and E variables, in terms of behavioral outcomes, are not yet known throughout the score ranges. It may be, as it is with intellectual capacity (I.Q.) in educational research: college applicants with scores below a cutting-point are likely to fail but, above the cutting-point, factors other than I.Q. become more important in predicting academic behavior [16]. In similar fashion, capacity may powerfully determine outcomes of P-E transactions for elderly persons below some yet-to-be-determined score or profile of scores, but of limited utility for persons within the "normal range" of score or score profile and in "normal" environments.

It is likely also that persons below some "incompetence threshold" comprise a relatively small proportion of the older population. Figures on institutionalization [17] and on adequate coping despite physical problems suggest that the large majority of elderly people are capable of dealing with non-malignant environments [18]. A general model must incorporate person traits relevant to the majority.

Capacity may act like a moderator variable, influencing the degree and kind of relationship between other variables [19, 20]. One of its roles in the general model may be to determine whether the defensive-adaptive or positive-adaptive aspect of the paradigm is appropriate. Below some threshold value, capacity may largely determine outcomes of P-E transactions, while above that threshold value capacity is of diminished importance and other P traits are more relevant.

For the activity sub-study, Housing Authority screening was accepted as documentation of adequate capacity to participate; the assumption was that, within this restricted range of capacity, need-satisfaction would account for significant amounts of variance in pre-post move change in behavior.

The role of needs—In regard to such behaviors as participation in activities on the part of independently living people, it seems essential to view the P in the Lewinian statement as more than a set of capacities, regardless of age. Matters of need and preference, for example, may be far more important. The fact that a person *can* play bridge, dance or do needlework does not mean that, given the opportunity, he inevitably will do so, or that doing so will increase his satisfaction with life.

Instead of conceptualizing behavior as the result of E demands upon P capacities, the model for this study emphasizes the importance of congruence between *P needs* and *E resources*. Such a model has respectable background in traditional psychological theory [3, 4, 21-25]. It seems that, in attending to the vulnerabilities of the frail elderly, most of the recent gerontological models of P-E interaction focus on the "defensive" aspect of the adaptation process to the neglect of the "positive adjustment" or "developmental" side. The general model for this study, like that of Kahana, posits gains in adaptation and satisfaction contingent upon improved need satisfaction through environmental intervention [26].

Latent demand for activity—In regard to activity, there is analogy with a "demand model" from the field of transportation [27, 28]. Transportation "demand" is defined in terms of overt behavior such as ridership rate. "Latent demand" is the rise in utilization predicted as consequence of some projected improvement in the transportation system; it is degree to which travel behavior (activity) is depressed by limitations in the transportation system (the environment). Validation of latent demand depends upon observation of the predicted rise in ridership following alteration of the transit environment.

In application to the present problem, latent demand is the predicted rise in activity level following the introduction of increased opportunities for activity; it is the difference in activity rate prior to addition of opportunities and subsequently. The basic assumption is that "latent demand for activity" existed: that the observed activity rates of applicants for housing were lower than what might be called the "rate of preference" or "rate of need" because of limitations in their environments. The basic hypothesis is that "demand," that is, activity rate, will rise in the presence of an environment which provides increased opportunity for activity.

Congruence—P-E congruence is important [26, 29, 30]. The prediction for the present study is not that expanded activity opportunities will uniformly increase activity among all old people, but only among community-resident persons "matched" to the new situation by the best efforts of a well-qualified staff and self-selected to it. The basic assumption is that the activities of elderly community-resident applicants for re-housing were curtailed by their environments: for persons in environments with limited opportunities for activity and who seek an alternative, "latent demand" for activities is high.

One hypothesis is that an environment which increases opportunity for activity will raise activity rates among such persons generally. To test this hypothesis it is appropriate to hold P constant and vary E; one way to do this is to move one group of similar persons to an environment with richer opportunities for activity while leaving the remainder in the same environment to comprise a comparison group. Due to the liklihood of intrinsic age-changes in activity rate, the test of the hypothesis is in terms of differential change over time between those in the activity-enriched environment and the others.

A relative matter—Age-related reduction in energy level and sensory-moter decrements suggest eventual reduction in activity for most persons who live to advanced age, but questions remain about timing and extent of activity diminution due to intrinsic changes. The question is not whether activity reduction is a normal consequence of growing old, but whether for some persons the environment forces inactivity prematurely. Taking into account age decrements in energy and sensory-motor functions, the hypothesis for the study is further specified: increase in activity rate (latent demand) is defined in relative rather than absolute terms: activity rates in the new environment were predicted to be higher than would be expected had the environment not been manipulated in regard to activity opportunities, as estimated by the behavior of comparison respondents.

Individual differences among movers—Furthermore, within the group exposed to the enriched environment, differences in proclivity for activity were predicted to influence behavioral outcomes. It was assumed for this purpose that need for activity was expressed in the limited-opportunity environment by relatively high activity rate and expressed desire for additional activity. It was hypothesized that, among movers, those with relatively high activity rates and those who expressed most interest in additional activities; as applicants, would be the VP tenants whose activity would increase most, while those originally least active and least interested in additional activities would show least rise or relative decrement in activity following the move.

Long-term effects and morale—Information to date has been on relatively short-range effects of changed housing and living arrangement; generally it supports the notion that both activity rate and life satisfaction rise following a move to prefered housing which also provides greater opportunity for activity [31-35]. Obviously the first year may be a poor index. Short-term rise in activity might be response to situational opportunity or to situational demand. To the extent that this initial burst of activity was not congruent with tenants' needs, fatigue would ultimately set in, along with other stress reactions, and activity rate and life satisfaction would decline. This report focuses on long-range changes.

It does not report results on morale, but changes in activity rate are interpreted here in light of knowledge that the new environment had favorable effect upon life satisfaction over the long run as well as the short [36]. There were other indications of improved well-being for those in the new situation. The milieu continued to be satisfactory which to its tenants, compared to their earlier dissatisfaction and the continued dissatisfaction of the comparison group [37]. Tenants' evaluation of their health were better, and mortality rate lower among them [38, 39]. This absence of evidence indicating stress among tenants of the new environment–indeed, the presence of considerable evidence indicative of reduced stress–suggest that the continuing response to the greater opportunity for activity expressed inner need. It is important to see, then, what that response was, after the "honeymoon" was over. Did activity rate remain elevated, did it revert to what it might have been without environmental intervention, or did it fall below that level?

Data

COLLECTION AND TREATMENT

Data regarding activities and use of time were collected in individual home interviews and, since information recorded day-by-day may be more accurate than that recalled, an activity diary was recorded by the interviewer for the preceding day, and each respondent was requested to keep a similar record for the following week. In various data collections the rate of return ranged from 64 per cent to 71 per cent. When the seven-day diary was not available the one-day record was used.

The applicants–Respondents at time-1 were 352 legally qualified applicants to Victoria Plaza (VP). Details regarding their characteristics have been reported [32]. In summary, 21 per cent were men and 79 per cent women. The average age was 72.24 when first contacted but most described themselves as "middle-aged." On demographic variables they were fairly typical for their age. They were poor (qualified for public housing) but their median income was nearly identical to that shown by the United States Census for elderly people on Social Security rolls. The range of income was restricted by Housing Authority standards, the upper limit by the legal requirements for eligibility and the lower by the necessity to pay at least minimum rent.[1] Though probably above average

[1] This pre-dated the Brooke Amendment which eliminated the minimum rent requirement.

in intelligence as measured by standardized tests (Verbal I.Q. on the Wechsler Scale of Adult Intelligence was 112 for a sample of 104), they were no better educated than others of their generation (typically eighth grade).

Their housing—The typical applicant lived in an "apartment" which was usually one small room partitioned out of a larger one on the second or third floor on in the attic of an old house. These living units typically served to inhibit participation in activities. There was little to do within the buildings and access to facilities outside them was difficult. The stairs constituted major obstacles, often being dimly lit and covered with frayed and worn carpeting. The neighborhood ordinarily offered little for old people to do, and conditions justified their fears of being on the street. For the minority in physically adequate housing the situation was one of crushing loneliness and wounding interpersonal relationships sufficiently serious to meet Housing Authority standards, which meant that they were unequivocal and well documented.

Victoria Plaza—This nine-story building contains eight residential floors with a total of 184 dwelling units, and usually has about 220 tenants. Elevators provide access between residential floors and to the lobby, which opens to the outside world with a bus stop at the nearest corner, and to the senior center which is the building's ground-floor tenant. (For a description of the center, see [12]).

Inmovers and others—Two hundred and four legally qualified applicants moved to VP and 148 did not. Demographic differences between movers and nonmovers, as applicants, were minimal even on admission standards [32], and there were no premove differences on the activity items used in this paper. When VP had been open a year, time-2 data were collected from 190 of the original group who were still tenants and 105 of the original group of legally qualified applicants who had not lived there. After eight years, time-3 data were obtained on 127 surviving VP tenants and sixty-two surviving comparison respondents.

Tests of change in activity—Change over time among VP tenants was compared to change among comparison respondents using regression model analysis of covariance for continuous and ordered variables [40-42] and the McNemar Change Test for dichotomous variables [43]. These statistics assess change among residents by comparing it with change among similar people who did not experience the environmental intervention and who, therefore, provide an estimate of what might have been expected for VP tenants, had they not moved. The regression model also assesses the influence of the value of the original score on each variable, allowing test of the hypothesis regarding differential impact of expanded opportunity upon activity according to inital level of activity.

Results

GROUP DIFFERENCES

The first hypothesis was that movers would be more active, relative to nonmovers, either by gain or by less loss, over time. This general hypothesis was tested using several variables.

"Regular responsibility"—In each interview, work history and status were recorded, as was commitment of time and effort on a regular and scheduled basis but for no pay. In view of the different roles of paid and unpaid "regular responsibilities" in adjustment to the new living environment at the end of the first year [30], the two were treated separately in the present analysis. Since VP offered no job opportunities, no difference was predicted for work activity. Since job opportunity in the community would become increasingly unavailable to persons in this age cohort, the expectaion was for too few workers to enable statistical testing. At time-3 no resident was working full-time though one nonresident man was. Four men who lived in the Plaza and two women who lived elsewhere had part-time jobs.

Living in VP did make available non-paid "regular responsibilities," both "building duties" such as host/hostess at the lobby desk and in connection with the senior center. As predicted, more VP tenants continued to be responsible for some regularly scheduled volunteer duty. (See Table 1) Twice as many tenants had some regular duty in connection with religious services, and a few tenants but no nontenants had some other community or charity responsibility on a continuing basis and a regular schedule: but this participation involved

Table 1. Differential Change Between Movers and Nonmovers Over 8 Years

Activity Variable	*Chi-square*	*F*
Regular Responsibility	18.60[a]	
Number of Pastimes		16.64[a]
% Active Pastimes		21.01[a]
Time Passive		13.96[a]
Time "lost"		27.09[a]
Time at T.V.		8.91[a]
Time at Meetings		11.04[a]
Activity Compared to 55	8.91[a]	
Desired Activities: Na	15.08[a]	

[a]Significant at or beyond .01 level
N for VP tenants 127
N for comparison group = 62

small numbers. The major contributor to difference in the "unpaid regular responsibility" variable was volunteer duty in VP and its senior center. At time-3, a quarter of the tenant respondents but no member of the comparison group served as host/hostess at the lobby desk, and 6 per cent of the residents had other "building duties."

Leisure pastimes: Activity checklist scores—During each interview a list of leisure pastimes was presented in written form and orally, and the respondent was asked to identify those in which he had participated frequently during the past six months. This information produced two scores relevant to this analysis: total number of pastimes (N Pt) and percentage of pastimes which were active (% Pt Act). The latter was computed on the basis of pre-assignment of each pastime as active or passive by three clinical psychologists working independently; the few activities on which all three did not agree were excluded. The score was the percentage of pastimes named which had been pre-coded "active." Predictions for gain or less loss on both scores among VP tenants relative to nontenants were supported. From time-1 to time-3 the tendency was toward increment among tenants and decrement among comparison respondents. Since initial scores were similar, comparisons at time-3 can exemplify the differences. At the end of eight years, the average number of leisure pastimes was 15 for the VP group but 8 for the others, and the percentages of active pastimes were 69 per cent and 56 per cent.

Component items provide the flavor of differences these scores represent. At time-3, nearly two-thirds of VP tenants (62%) has participated in club meetings during the past six months compared to just over a quarter (27%) of their counterparts. Many more (45% to 8%) played table games. More VP residents read (75% to 34%), went visiting (72% to 62%), wrote letters (47% to 23%), gardened (23% to 12%), and attended theaters and plays (10% to 4%). The following pastimes were reported by no member of the comparison group, while participation among VP tenants was: community service or charity work, (28%); painting, (19%); crafts, (14%); singing, (11%); putting on skits, (10%); going to movies, (10%); attending football or baseball games, (10%); discussion groups, (8%); lectures, (8%); playing musical instruments, (8%); book reviews, (7%); concerts, (7%); school, (6%); dancing, (4%): modeling (clothes!), (4%); writing books or articles, (3%).

Most members of both groups reported napping and resting as a "leisure pastime" and the incidence increased for both, but somewhat less among VP tenants. At time-3, 90 per cent of them compared to 100 per cent of the comparison respondents mentioned napping and resting as an habitual use of leisure time. The pastime most clearly more prevalent among comparison respondents was "just sitting." (This was separate from "sitting and thinking.") At the final data collection less than half (47%) of the VP tenants but well over three-quarters (81%) of non-tenants reported "just sitting" as a common pastime during the preceding six months.

Activity diaries—To develop scoring categories for the activity diaries, two graduate students in psychology were given copies of cards, each of which contained one entry from a time diary, and were instructed to sort them into piles according to similarity. All time-1 and time-2 entries were included. Disagreements tended to be in the number of "independent" categoreis and were resolved in conference with the author, usually in the direction of fewer categories. A series of sortings, discussions and resortings were necessary to produce a set of categories which seemed adequate. To insure consistency, scoring instructions were prepared which named and defined each category and provided examples of items. Those about which there had been difference of opinion were included as examples.

To eliminate "halo" due to knowledge of who was in the "treatment" and comparison groups, or from one response to another for the same respondent, scoring was also done from cards, each of which showed only one response item and which had been shuffled, rather than from intact protocols. Scoring was done by two graduate students who had not been involved in category development. Disagreements, which occurred in regard to less than 1 per cent of the items,[2] were resolved by the two scorers, working together. These problematic items were added to the scoring manual as examples. A respondent's score on each category was the average time per day, to the nearest quarter hour, he spent in that use of time.

Hypotheses were that tenants would show less increment in passive use of time, sleeping, "lost" time, and time spent on television; and relative gain (gain or less loss) in time spent at meetings. Trends over time supported the predictions. Across the eight years residents showed less gain in amount of time during which they "just sat" (not including "sat and thought") or "did nothing"; and there was smaller increment in time for which they could not account, "lost time" during which they recorded nothing and were unable to recall what they had been doing. For example, at time-3, VP residents averaged less than an hour, while comparison respondents averaged nearly three hours a day "just sitting" or "doing nothing" in addition to the time for which they could not account. A composite score which included time spent napping, "just sitting" or "doing nothing," and "lost time" showed a highly significant difference over time between groups, with greater increase among nontenants. Time spent by VP tenants at meetings was three times that for others, while time spent on T.V. was about two-thirds as much as time-3.

Present activity compared to past—During each interview people were asked whether their current rate of activity was more, less or about the same as when

[2]The very high inter-rater agreement is due not only to the objectivity of the scoring system but also to the repetitiveness of time-diary entries (e.g., slept, ate breakfast, watched T.V.).

they were fifty-five years old. Trends over time were predicted to be different for VP tenants and others, with less loss on the part of the former. This prediction was supported. For example, from a similar response distribution at baseline for the two groups, at time-3 over a quarter (27%) of VP tenants compared to only 7 per cent of other respondents said their current rate of participation in activities was "more" than at age fifty-five while 18 per cent of the tenants but a third of the non-tenants said it was "less."

Future activity–Each interview included a section on leisure pastimes in which one would like to participate if circumstances permitted. Hypotheses parallelled those regarding current participation: VP tenants were predicted to gain (or lose less) relative to nontenants in the total number of activities desired and the percentage of desired activities pre-coded as active.

At time-3 the large majority of people outside VP chose to skip this section or answered "I don't know" to all or most items. The common justification is summed up by one comment: "it is foolish for me to think of things like that because it won't happen." The low rate of response from comparison respondents precludes statistical comparison regarding number and kinds of activities in which people would like to take part if circumstances permitted, but the pervasive avoidance among the comparison group seems meaningful in itself. The difference between groups in incidence of "no answer" to this series of questions was statistically significant.

INDIVIDUAL DIFFERENCES AMONG MOVERS

It was hypothesized that P-E congruence would vary among movers, and that applicants with greatest proclivity for an active life-style would make greatest use of the expanded opportunity for activity. This hypothesis was tested in two ways: by predicting time-2 and time-3 activity rate on the basis of time-1 desire for activity, and by regressing post-move scores upon pre-move scores for continuous and ordered activity variables.

Desire for activity–The number of activity checklist items named at baseline as desired if conditions permitted was a reasonably good predictor of the number of leisure activities, using the same checklist, at time-2 ($r = .54$) and time-3 ($r = .41$).

Original activity level–Furthermore, the value of the original score affected the change in behavior in the environment having greater activity opportunity, in the case of every activity variable. (See Table 2) Generally people more active as applicants showed greater gain in activity following the move. Regression lines relating pre- and post-move scores for number of pastimes, percentage of active pastimes, and time spent at meetings all have positive intercepts and positive slopes, indicating general score gain and greater gain for those with high

Table 2. Individual Differences in Change Among Movers

Activity Variable	*Slope*	*Intercept*	*a/d*
Number of pastimes	> 1	+	
% Pastime active	> 1	+	
Time passive + lost	> 1	–	x
Time at T.V.	< 1	+	x
Time at meetings	> 1	+	

Note: Departure of the slope from 1 and of the intercept from 0 were tested with the F statistic and were significant at the .01 level. Results are presented in schematic form because numeric values differ for time-1 to time-2 and for time-1 to time-3 change. However, change over both intervals followed the patterns shown above.
N = 127

original scores, over both time intervals (time-1 to time-2 and time-1 to time-3). (For fuller description of the data analysis model see reference [40]).

The regression lines for the activity diary score incorporating time spent passively, sleeping and "lost" showed positive slopes and negative intercepts, and "cross-over" (a/d) values.[3] This means that for most movers (80%-85% had pre-test scores below the cross-over value), time passive or "lost" decreased; and the smaller the initial score, the greater the decrease. However, for the minority with initial scores above the a/d value, lost and passive time tended to increase; and the larger the original score, the greater the increase. These results suggest that, while expanded activity resource was reflected in more active and more purposeful use of time on the part of most persons who chose it, the same environmental opportunity (or perhaps "demand") was reflected in increased passivity, sleep and "lost" time on the part of the minority who originally scored high on this variable.

Television viewing for VP tenants was represented by regression lines with negative slopes and positive intercepts, and which had cross-over values. For VP tenants with pre-move scores smaller than the a/d values, there was increment during each time interval, and the less the original time at T.V., the greater the increment; for those with original scores above the cross-over values there was diminution, and the larger the initial score the greater the reduction. In other words, for those who as applicants watched T.V. a great deal, viewing time decreased following the move; and the greater the original time, the larger the decrement. For those who, as applicants, watched T.V. little or none, there was increase, and the smaller the original viewing time, the greater the increment. This tendency, not accounted for by statistical regression toward the mean, suggests conformity to the social mores of the new living environment.

[3] This is the baseline score value, x_1, for which $a \pm dx_1 = 0$, $x_1 = a/d$, where a is the intercept and d is the amount by which the slope differs from 1. Generally, the more extreme an individual's original score from this value, the greater was the change in his score over time.

Summary and Implications

Living in VP—where formal activities were offered by the tenant organization and in the senior center, and opportunities for informal activities abounded—maintained activity at a higher level than it would otherwise have been, for the group as a whole. Differences between VP residents and other members of the original group of legally qualified applicants remained consistent even at the end of eight years, documenting a "latent demand" for activity among applicants. This relative maintenance of activity level was accompanied by greater satisfaction with the living environment [37], greater life satisfaction and better morale [36], better self-evaluations of health and increased longevity [38, 39]. The concurrence of activity with morale and longevity further suggest that the environmental arrangements which enabled and supported activity were need-meeting.

Care must be taken in generalizing from these data. This was a special group of people and a particular type of environment in which they chose to live. They were self-selected as well as qualified for admission by experts. The applicant group not only needed housing and were capable of independent living there, they also were attracted by what they knew of VP. Despite their resemblance to old people in general on demographic items, applicants revealed an unusual level of knowledge about the community by being aware of the new facility, and considerable wit and temerity by completing application to it. The average I.Q. of those tested was above normal. There may be personality differences; population descriptions are not available to permit testing of this possiblity.

The need for caution in generalizing is accentuated by analysis of data on movers, which demonstrated interaction between P and E, differential impact of E according to individual differences among Ps. In general, applicants who were more active and who expressed interest in additional specific activities showed greatest gains in activity after moving; while the new environment seemed to confirm inactivity on the part of those originally least active.

The data document the existence of "latent demand" for activity within the community-resident elderly population and indicate that environmental intervention can increase activity rate among older people over what it would have been otherwise. Since better life satisfaction and life expectancy accompanied this higher level of activity, it seems safe to conclude also that—for intact people who choose it—a living environment which provides for and expects an active life-style can be a beneficial setting in which to grow old. The findings also confirm the importance of individual differences and of person-environment congruence in determining outcomes.

REFERENCES

1. J. L. Rosen and B. L. Neugarten, Ego Functions in the Middle and Later Years: A Thematic Apperception Study of Normal Adults, *Journal of Gerontology, 15,* pp. 62-67, 1960.
2. F. M. Carp, Impact of Improved Housing Upon Social Activity and Interpersonal Relationships, in press a.
3. K. Lewin, (D.K. Adams and K. E. Zener, trans.), *A Dynamic Theory of Personality,* McGraw-Hill, Inc., New York, 1935.
4. H. A. Murray, *Explorations in Personality,* Oxford University Press, New York, 1938.
5. L. A. Pervin, Performance and Satisfaction as a Function of Individual-Environment Fit, in R. H. Moos and P. M. Insel (eds.), *Issues in Social Ecology,* National Press Books, Palo Alto, 1974.
6. M. P. Lawton, Coping Behavior and the Environment of Older People, in A. N. Schwartz and I. N. Mensh (eds.), *Professional Obligation and Approaches to the Aged,* Charles C. Thomas, Springfield, Ill., 1974.
7. M. P. Lawton, Competence, Environmental Press and the Adaptation of Older People, in P. Windley, T. C. Byerts and G. Ernst (eds.), *Theory Development in Environment and Aging,* Gerontological Society, Washington, D.C., 1975.
8. M. P. Lawton and L. Nahemow, Ecology and Adaptation in the Aging Process, in C. Eisdorfer and M. P. Lawton (eds.), *Psychology of the Aging Process,* American Psychological Association, Washington, D.C., 1973.
9. M. P. Lawton and B. Simon, The Ecology of Social Relationships in Housing for the Elderly, *The Gerontologist, 8,* pp. 108-115, 1968.
10. L. Nahemow and M. P. Lawton, Toward an Ecological Theory of Adaptation and Aging, in W. Preiser (ed.), *Environmental Design Research, 1,* Dowden Hutchinson & Ross, Stroudsburg, Pa., 1973.
11. F. M. Carp, User Evaluation of Housing for the Elderly, *The Gerontologist, 16:2,* pp. 105-111, 1976 a.
12. _____ A Senior Center in Public Housing for the Elderly, *The Gerontologist, 16:3,* pp. 243-249, 1976 b.
13. C. S. Hall and G. Lindzey, *Theories of Personality,* J. Wiley & Sons, Inc., New York, 1957.
14. M. Merleau-Ponty, (A. L. Fisher, trans.), *The Structure of Behavior,* Beacon Press, Boston, 1967.
15. W. H. Ittelson, H. M. Proshansky, L. G. Rivlin and G. H. Winkel, *An Introduction to Environmental Psychology,* Holt, Rinehart and Winston, New York, 1974.
16. Krech and R. S. Crutchfield, *Elements and Psychology,* A. L. Knopf, New York, 1969.
17. H. Brotman, Every Tenth American-The "Problem" of Aging, M. P. Lawton, R. J. Newcomer and T. O. Byerts (eds.), *Community Planning for the Elderly,* Dowden, Hutchinson and Ross, Stroudsburg, Penn., pp. 5-18, 1976.
18. R. J. Havighurst, Research and Development Goals in Social Gerontology, *The Gerontologist, 9:4,* 1969.

19. R. M. Guion, *Personnel Testing,* McGraw-Hill, New York, 1965.
20. D. R. Saunders, Moderator Variables in Prediction, *Educational Psychology Measurement, 16,* pp. 209-222, 1956.
21. A. H. Maslow, *Motivation and Personality,* Harper, New York, 1954.
22. E. H. Erikson, *Childhood and Society,* W.W. Norton & Co., Inc., 1950.
23. R. W. White, Motivation Reconsidered: The Concept of Competence, *Psychological Review,* LXVI pp. 297-333, 1959.
24. G. W. Allport, *Becoming: Basic Considerations for a Psychology of Personality,* Yale University Press, New Haven, 1955.
25. S. Freud, (E. Van Teslaar, ed.), *An Outline of Psycho-Analysis,* Modern Library, Inc., New York, 1924.
26. E. Kahana, A Congruence Model of Person Environment Interaction, in M. P. Lawton and T. Byerts (eds.), *Theoretical Approaches to the Study of Environments and Aging,* John Wiley & Sons, Inc., New York, 1975.
27. D. L. McFadden, The Theory and Measurement of Qualitative Consumer Behavior: The Case of Urban Travel Demand, *BART–I Final Report Series,* Institute for Urban and Regional Development, University of California, Berkeley, 1973a.
28. D. L. McFadden, Conditional Logic Analysis of Qualitative Choice Behavior, *BART–I Final Report Series,* Institute for Urban and Regional Development, University of California, Berkeley, 1973 b.
29. F. M. Carp, Person-situation Congruence in Engagement, *The Gerontologist, 8,* pp. 184-188, 1968 a.
30. _____ Differences Among Older Workers, Volunteers and Persons Who are Neither, *Journal of Gerontology, 23,* pp. 497-501, 1968 b.
31. G. L. Bultena and V. Wood, The American Retirement Community: Bane or Blessing?, *Journal of Gerontology, 24,* pp. 209-217, 1969.
32. F. M. Carp, *A Future for the Aged,* University of Texas Press, Austin, 1966.
33. W. Donahue, Impact of Living Arrangements on Ego Development in the Elderly, in F. M. Carp (ed.), *Patterns of Living and Housing of Middle-Aged and Older People,* United States Government Printing Office, Washington, D.C., 1966.
34. M. B. Hamovitch, Social and Psychological Factors in Adjustment in a Retirement Village, in F. M. Carp (ed.), *The Retirement Process,* United States Government Printing Office, Washington, D.C., 1968.
35. M. P. Lawton and J. Cohen, Housing impact on Older People, *Journal of Gerontology, 2,* pp. 194-294, 1974.
36. F. M. Carp, Impact of Improved Housing on Morale and Life Satisfaction, *The Gerontologist, 15:6,* pp. 511-515, 1975 a.
37. _____ Long-range Satisfaction with Housing, *The Gerontologist, 15:1,* pp. 68-72, 1975 b.
38. _____ Housing and Living Arrangements, in L. E. Brown and E. O. Ellis (eds.), *Quality of Life: The Later Years,* Publishing Sciences Group, Action, Massachusetts, pp. 168-173, 1975 c.
39. _____ Impact of Improved Living Environment on Health and Life Expectancy, *The Gerontologis, 17:3,* pp. 242-249, 1977.

40. _____ A Regression Model for Longitudinal Assessment of Treatment Effect, in press b.
41. J. D. Finn, *A General Model for Multivariate Analysis,* Holt, Reinhart & Winston, New York, 1974.
42. I. Kerlinger and E. Pedhazur, *Multiple Regression in Behavioral Research,* Holt, Reinhart & Winston, New York, 1973.
43. McNemar, *Psychological Statistics,* (3rd ed.), John Wiley & Sons, Inc., New York, 1962.

chapter 9

THE ECOLOGY OF ADAPTATION TO A NEW ENVIRONMENT*

M. Powell Lawton
Beverly Patnaik
Morton H. Kleban

The way people distribute themselves in space, like any other behavior, must be assumed to be purposeful. Yet, it is a relatively recent phenomenon to have been studied by the methods of social science, beginning with geography and now including the broad interdisciplinary science of man-environment relations [1-3]. Such behavior as crowding [4], the search for privacy [5], the distancing of people in relation to one another [6], and the choice of specific locations for specific behaviors [7] have been studied by anthropologists, sociologists and psychologists both as the cause of other behaviors and as the result of antecedent conditions. The broadest view of such behavior sees it as a part of the total behavioral system, where human needs not only are satisfied in a particular location, but may be blocked or facilitated by the use of space, objects, and other people in the space. Furthermore, the individual

* A revision of a paper presented at the annual meeting of the Gerontological Society, Miami Beach, November 7, 1973 and supported by Grant HS00100, from the Health Services and Mental Health Administration.

is seen as utilizing space in a characteristic style that is consonant with his behavior in other spheres.

The present study examines some aspects of the use of space and objects by people faced with the demand to adapt to an environmental change not of their own choosing. The most general hypothesis was that they would alter such spatial behavior in a manner that would help them deal with an ostensibly stressful experience.

The occasion for the study was the intra-institutional room transfer of twenty-four residents of a longterm care institution for the elderly, which required the vacating of twenty-four other room spaces—a total of forty-eight residents requiring relocation. The moves were mandated by implementation in Pennsylvania of Public Law 92-603 as of January 1, 1973. Longterm care thereby was placed under Title 19 of the Social Security Act instead of under Public Assistance as had been the case prior to that date. Separate and distinct areas for the categories of skilled nursing care and intermediate care were required, each with its own specified uniform staffing pattern and level of reimbursement. Prior to January 1, the monthly maintenance charge was uniform throughout the institution, but residents were grouped in five different areas in accordance with their need for care. The staffing patterns of the areas had varied appropriately. The net effect of the change would be homogenization of residents and more even distribution of staff within the two broad levels ("skilled" and "intermediate"). The skilled nursing care area, of course, was to be for residents requiring more skilled nursing care than those in the intermediate area, and the staffing requirements are greater. The homogenization was thus accomplished by transferring some relatively independent residents to floors that had been serving the more dependent residents, and vice-versa. The relocation was accomplished after a period of careful planning by the entire staff of the institution, working together with both residents and their families. The forty-eight moves were made on a single day, with the mobilization of the entire staff, particular care being taken in such matters as counseling, preparation and support of the movers, moving familiar furniture, scheduling elevator use, and reorienting the resident to his new surroundings. Whatever could have been done to moderate the well-documented stress of environmental change was accomplished.

This relocation was utilized as a natural experiment by the social work and behavioral science research staffs. While there have been many studies of relocation between institutions [8-10], and of housing relocation [11, 12], the only studies of relocation within an institution have utilized younger mental patients [13, 14], and none of these has dealt explicitly with the effects of the relocation on spatial behavior.

The institutional milieu is known to minimize opportunities for privacy and to restrict grossly the range of space and objects that are definable as one's own. Whatever territory can become personalized is jealously guarded, and a variety of compensatory means of establishing one's private world are utilized:

the staking out of a chair, or part of a public room as one's own; the exchange of avoidance behaviors with a roommate; or the "turning off" of interactive behavior in a crowded public space [15]. The attachment to one's own room or floor is a part of such attempts to preserve the self in both a psychological and a spatial sense. An essential ingredient of this state of institutional adjustment is clear knowledge of where such things as furniture, staff offices, bathrooms, exits, and familiar faces are located. Thus, the loss of these sources of stability would be expected to activate new behaviors and new uses of space whose purpose would be to minimize the stress of the change.

We hypothesized that behavior would change in such a way as:

1. to maximize the opportunity for reorientation to a new environment and
2. to minimize the risk of anxiety-arousing consequences of too-sudden exposure to new environmental stimuli.

Method

SUBJECTS

Of the total of forty-eight residents being relocated, eleven from the first floor of the institution were exchanged with a similar number from the topmost floor, and thirteen others were shifted from one first-floor room to another on the same floor. With very little time to plan the study and to gather data, it was decided to limit the study to these two physical areas, involving the majority of the relocations. The total number of residents moving to or within the first floor was thirty-one (including seven from the other floors not mapped), while eleven moved to the top floor. Individual assessment of the relocated residents in terms of health and functional capacity could not be performed within the time limits. However, the net effect of the moves was clearly to populate the first floor with more independent residents than it previously housed, and conversely for the top floor. The total resident bed census on the first floor was fifty-four, on the top floor seventy-four.

PROCEDURE

The data reported here were gathered exclusively from direct observation of the behavior occurring in the two physical areas of the institution, in the form of behavior maps [16]. A map of the entire floor was reproduced, and the position and behavior of every individual noted by research assistants trained in the mapping technique. The observer began at a predetermined point on the floor and followed a prescribed routine of gazing successively at each area of the ward, walking or pausing as required to be able to code the following individual behavior.

Individual characteristics–All residents were mapped whether the person was a resident, staff member, volunteer, or visitor and regardless of whether or not they were involved in the move. Individuals were not identified by name.

Physical location of the individual–Each person's location was marked on the map, but for coding, locations were classified as bedroom, hall (closed end), hall (nearest the elevator and exit), and lounge.

Position of the individual–Each person's position was noted as lying down, sitting, standing, walking (with or without cane or walker), in wheelchair (self-propelled) or in wheelchair (being pushed by another person). For analysis, walking and wheelchair ambulation were considered a single category.

Behavior of the individual–Behavior was classified as social, effectance (i.e., non-obligatory constructive behaviors such as reading, watching TV, engaging in occupational therapy, and so on), instrumental (eating, dressing, housekeeping for example), sleeping, or null behavior (the apparent absence of any activity, though awake). Since walking was both a position and a behavior, those who were walking appear only in the totals for positions.

The observer thus attempted to obtain a photographic image of the total pattern of behavior, though the picture had to be composed in serial fashion over time. The time required to do each behavior map was about 30 minutes. All areas of each floor were covered, except for resident and staff rooms whose doors were closed. A closed resident's door was treated as an item of data, but in order not to intrude further on the resident's privacy, no attempt was made to enter such rooms.

Behavior maps were done on two occasions:

1. During the two weeks before the move, before residents had been notified that they were to move. The last maps were done on the sixth day before the move.
2. During the two weeks following the move, beginning one day after the move took place. Five times of day were sampled: 9:00 A.M., 10:30 A.M., 1:00 P.M., 2:30 P.M. and 4:00 P.M.

An attempt was made to obtain equal numbers of maps for every time on each floor for each occasion, but because of problems in scheduling enough personnel time, there were thirty-nine maps done on the first and forty-three on the top floor prior to the move, and forty-five on both floors following the move.

Following the completion of the maps, each map was coded in terms of the number of residents and staff in each physical area, the number of open doors, the position of each resident, and the behavior each was observed to be engaged in at the time.

Results

TOTAL NUMBER OF RESIDENTS OBSERVED

One aspect of reorientation to a new environment by a person of low competence involves his restricting his behavioral range, that is, remaining close to his home territory. Therefore, we expected that more residents would be counted on the floor area following the move. The mean number of residents observed on each mapping on the first floor prior to the move was 16.9, and following the move 18.3. This difference was not significant ($t = 1.39$, 83 df, $p > .05$). On the top floor the pre-move mean of 10.4 did not differ significantly from the post-move mean, 11.8 ($t = 1.40$, 87 df, $p > .05$).

OPEN DOORS

Another aspect of reorientation is the need to survey the new environment—to gain a maximum amount of information about the physical and social aspects of life in a new location. We thus hypothesized that relocated residents would be more likely to leave their doors open, so as to be able both to survey activity in the hall from their rooms and also to be able to monitor their own rooms from a position outside of the room. We also reasoned that non-movers would experience heightened interest in what went on after such a major change in the complexion of their floors. Since it was easy to determine which rooms housed any resident who was to move, separate counts of open doors were made for "affected" (i.e., rooms containing a mover) and "unaffected" (rooms containing no movers) rooms. Table 1 shows the excess of open doors in the post-move as compared to the pre-move occasion at each time period for each floor, with separate totals for affected

Table 1. Percentage Excess of Open Doors on Post-Move as Compared Pre-Move Condition at Five Observation Occasions

	First Floor		*Fourth Floor*	
	Affected rooms	*Unaffected rooms*	*Affected rooms*	*Unaffected rooms*
9:00 AM	13	11	11	4
10:30 AM	23	14	10	3
1:00 PM	12	14	7	1
2:30 PM	8	12	13	6
4:00 PM	11	- 2	9	1

p (affected rooms) = .00097.
p (unaffected rooms) = .0039.

and unaffected rooms. It can be seen that while differences were sometimes small, the predicted relationship occurred 10 times out of 10 occasions in the affected rooms ($p = .001$ by the binomial test) and 9 out of 10 occasions for the unaffected rooms ($p = .004$).

Location of Body Position and Behavior of Staff and Residents

The percentage distributions of staff and residents observed on all behavior maps both prior to and following the move are shown in Table 2, using as a base the total number of residents or staff observed over all occasions (the infrequently-occurring staff categories are omitted). The significance of the differences between the pre- and post-relocation percentages was calculated by z scores, shown in Table 2; a negative z indicates that the pre-location percentage was higher. One-tailed tests were used where the category had been hypothesized to change in a particular direction; otherwise, two-tailed tests were used.

We hypothesized that more passive behavior would be the dominant response to the dislocation, on the theory that these relatively dependent residents would attempt to conserve energy and avoid immediate entry into more demanding and complex types of behavior. Specifically, we expected that residents would be:

1. more likely to be found in bedrooms rather than in halls, common spaces or in the vicinity of the nurses station;
2. more likely to be lying down, sitting, or standing, than walking; and
3. more likely to exhibit null behavior and sleeping, rather than instrumental, effectant, or social behavior.

Predictions for staff were roughly that the reverse would be true, namely that the demands of coping with the residents' relocation would result in more active behavior. However, for location, it was thought that if staff's locational patterns changed, they would change in the same direction that residents' patterns would change, since presumably some of the additional job-related tasks would require them to be with residents wherever they were.

RESIDENTS' PATTERNS

Examination of Table 2 reveals the following:

Location–On the first floor, lounge population decreased significantly, as was predicted, while bedroom population increased on both floors. The busiest part of the hall on the top floor decreased in population, with the same effect barely missing significance on the lower floor. No change occurred in the population of the closed end of the hall.

Table 2. Percentages of Persons Observed in Floor Locations, Body Positions and Engaging in Various Behaviors

	First Floor			*Top Floor*		
	Pre-move	*Post-move*	*Z*	*Pre-move*	*Post-move*	*Z*
Residents						
Location						
Lounge	44.7	32.7	-4.81[b]	25.7	23.5	-0.81
Bedrooms	21.7	38.7	7.00[b]	17.5	27.0	3.57[b]
Hall (closed end)	9.1	7.6	-1.04	17.2	16.3	-0.39
Hall (elevator end)	24.6	21.0	-1.64	39.5	33.2	-2.06[a]
Total observed	100.1 (N = 651)	100.0 (N = 829)		99.9 (N = 463)	100.0 (N = 533)	
Position						
Lying down	4.4	9.3	3.50[b]	2.9	3.4	0.45
Sitting	56.0	51.9	-1.54	40.7	46.0	1.67
Standing	10.5	15.2	2.60[b]	22.4	21.3	-0.42
Walking	29.1	23.5	-2.54[b]	34.1	29.4	-1.58
Total observed	100.0 (N = 621)	99.9 (N = 816)		100.1 (N = 455)	100.1 (N = 531)	
Behavior						
Null	17.3	21.9	1.89[a]	16.1	22.1	2.02[b]
Sleep	16.2	15.1	-0.49	8.0	7.9	-0.04
Instrumental	5.3	11.3	3.50[b]	7.1	11.2	1.87
Effectance	35.0	25.7	-3.33[b]	22.6	19.3	-1.08
Social	26.1	26.0	-0.04	46.1	39.4	-1.81[a]
Total observed	99.9 (N = 468)	100.0 (N = 627)		99.9 (N = 323)	99.9 (N = 393)	

Table 2. (Cont.)

	First Floor			Top Floor		
	Pre-move	*Post-move*	*Z*	*Pre-move*	*Post-move*	*Z*
Staff						
Location						
Lounge	12.7	12.1	-0.24	3.9	3.6	-0.14
Bedrooms	4.2	8.7	2.41[b]	7.2	14.3	2.05[b]
Hall (closed end)	24.8	25.4	0.18	18.3	28.6	2.24[a]
Hall (elevator end)	58.3	53.8	-1.19	70.6	53.6	-3.23[b]
Total observed	100.0 (N = 355)	100.0 (N = 3411)		100.0 (N = 153)	100.1 (N = 196)	
Position						
Sitting	11.9	13.7	0.72	19.0	18.6	-0.09
Standing	10.0	11.5	0.65	54.0	58.8	0.88
Walking	78.1	74.7	-1.08	27.0	22.5	-0.95
Total observed	100.0 (N = 360)	99.9 (N = 204)		100.0 (N = 137)	99.9 (N = 204)	
Behavior						
Instrumental	14.2	19.6	1.18	31.7	42.5	1.75[a]
Social	85.8	80.4	-1.18	68.3	57.5	-1.75
Total observed	100.0 (N = 127)	100.0 (N = 148)		100.0 (N = 109)	100.0 (N = 146)	

[a] *P* .05.
[b] *P* .01.

Position–On the first floor, three hypothesized changes occurred: An increase in the percentage lying down and standing, and a decrease in the percentage walking. On the fourth floor, there was a marginal increase in the percentage sitting.

Behavior–On the first floor, the hypothesized increase in null behavior and decrease in effectance occurred to a significant degree, while on the fourth floor, null behavior increased and social behavior decreased, as hypothesized. We hypothesized that instrumental behavior would also decrease, on the theory that greater passivity should be reflected in all behaviors. To the contrary, instrumental behavior increased significantly on the top floor (two-tailed test).

STAFF PATTERNS

Location–In conformity with our expectation, staff population in resident bedrooms increased on both floors, indicating that they tended to be wherever residents needed them. The same parallelism was seen in the decreased staff population of the elevator end of the hall on the top floor. Staff also showed a significant redistribution into the closed end of the hall on the top floor, which did not parallel any resident trend (two-tailed test).

Position–No significant changes were found in the distribution of staff over the three relevant body positions.

Behavior–Only two types of staff behavior occurred with great enough frequency to be analyzed. The heavy preponderance of social behavior results from the arbitrary restriction of categorizing each behavior only once; much staff activity involved simultaneous instrumental and social behavior, in which case the more complex (i.e., social) was tallied. The instrumental behavior increase on the top floor was expected since residents had shown a similar increase; this difference was significant using a one-tailed test. The complementary decrease in social behavior, while it paralleled resident behavior, was not covered by a hypothesis, and therefore, even though z was, naturally, the same size as the z for instrumental behavior, application of the two-tailed test left this value short of significance.

Discussion

Out of all predictions made regarding changes in residents' behavior twelve were supported, thirteen were not, and one changed significantly in a direction opposite to that predicted. The twelve supported predictions indicate very strongly the increase in passive types of behavior and space occupancy. The very clearcut findings showing more open bedroom doors following the relocation support the idea that a first task for the relocated is to re-establish their orientation to their physical and social surroundings.

Almost as interesting as the predicted effects was the one that ran opposite to prediction: the increase in instrumental behavior that occurred on one floor and barely missed significance on the other floor. Most observed instrumental behavior occurred in the resident's room: grooming, housekeeping, washing, and so on. Important among these behaviors were rearranging one's possessions, tidying clothes, and so on, tasks that were specific to being in a new location. Thus, though this interpretation is necessarily a *post hoc* conclusion, one gets the larger picture of a relatively adaptive response to a most stressful change. While restriction of behavioral range and greater passivity are generally considered undesirable behaviors over the long run, they may well have allowed the individuals to reconstitute their resources for future more active dealings with their environment. The open doors and other signs of reorientation are necessary preludes to later increased mobility. The increase in instrumental behavior was not only appropriate to the personal rearrangements that go with any move, but also indicates the residents' continued ability to be active in a safe, spatially-restricted way.

Making this argument for the positive adaptive quality of the behavior changes seen immediately after moving implies additionally that behavior should return to normal after the initial adjustment period. That is, a few months later, fewer bedroom doors should be open, there should be less null behavior, less sitting, less standing, and less bedroom use; there should be more effectance and social behavior, more walking, and more use of halls and lounges. Unfortunately, there was no way to test this hypothesized outcome, since the complexions of both floors continued to change as further transfers to and from these floors were made in the normal course of institutional management, this time spread out over time rather than being concentrated in a single day.

One is struck by the greater number of changes occurring on the first floor as compared to the top floor. We are inclined to attribute this to the fact that the total number of room changes on the first floor was much greater—again a further validation of the notion of a relocation effect. Very little seems explainable on the basis of simple change in the types of residents housed in the two areas. The net change in resident characteristics on the lower floor was toward higher competence and on the top floor toward lesser competence; yet, most changes in behavior and location on both floors were consistent with a lowered level of functioning, temporary though we believe it to be.

Finally, as might be expected, staff behavior changed less than resident behavior. Furthermore, in those five instances where it did change, it was always congruent with patient change, even if all such changes were not originally predicted. Thus, we can conclude that the less vulnerable group, staff, maintained more stable behavior and space-use patterns following the disruption, and that their competence was expressed in their alteration of behavior, where necessary, so as to be of maximum assistance to residents.

This study of the adaptation process in relatively dependent older people constitutes only one aspect of the more general problem of relocation as discussed with respect to migration of groups of all ages [17], of individual moving [18] and relatively healthy older people living in the community [19]. Passivity and cognitive restructuring are only two of the possible means that may be utilized. Beck, Cohen, Craik, Dwyer, McCleary, and Wapner [20] have discussed a number of possible adaptive styles that people may utilize in anticipation of a move, in the process of moving, and following a move. While Holmes and Holmes present evidence of the stressful quality of relocation for all people, there seems to be a greater effect on older people than on young [18]. This phenomenon seems consistent with the "environmental docility hypothesis" which suggests that the behavior of individuals of reduced competence (such as the mentally ill, aged, or economically deprived) is more susceptible to determination by environmental influences than is true for those of higher competence [21]. Further study of the conditions of environmental impact from the point of view of both individual and environment seems warranted in order to foresee, plan for, or minimize negative effects in a number of situations.

REFERENCES

1. J. Wohlwill, The Emerging Discipline of Environmental Psychology, *American Psychologist, 25,* pp. 303-312, 1970.
2. K. H. Craik, Environmental Psychology, in *New Directions in Psychology 4,* Holt, Rinehart & Winston, New York, 1970.
3. L. A. Pastalan and D. H. Carson, (eds.), *Spatial Behavior of Older People,* University of Michigan, Institute of Gerontology, Ann Arbor, 1970.
4. J. B. Calhoun, The Role of Space in Animal Sociology, *Journal of Social Issues, 22,* pp. 46-58, 1966.
5. N. Marshall, Environmental Components of Orientation Toward Privacy, in J. Archea and C. Eastman, (eds.), *EDRA 2,* Carnegie-Mellon University, Pittsburgh, 1970.
6. E. T. Hall, *The Hidden Dimension,* Doubleday, New York, 1966.
7. I. Altman, P. A. Nelson and E. E. Lett, *The Ecology of Home Environments,* Psychology Department, University of Utah, Salt Lake City, 1972 Final report, Grant OEG-8-70-0202, U.S. Office of Education, (Mimeo report).
8. C. K. Aldrich and E. Mendkoff, Relocation of the Aged and Disabled: A Mortality Study, *Journal of the American Geriatrics Society, 11,* pp. 185-194, 1963.
9. E. Markus, M. Blenkner, M. Bloom and T. Downs, The Impact of Relocation Upon Mortality Rates of Institutionalized Aged Persons, *Journal of Gerontology, 26,* pp. 537-541, 1971.
10. E. C. Killian, Effect of Geriatric Transfers on Mortality Rates, *Social Work, 15,* pp. 19-26, 1970.

11. F. M. Carp, *A Future for the Aged,* University of Texas Press, Austin, Texas, 1966.
12. M. P. Lawton and S. Yaffe, Mortality, Morbidity, and Voluntary Change of Residence by Older People, *Journal of the American Geriatrics Society, 18,* pp. 823-831, 1970.
13. M. Zlotowski and D. Cohen, Effects of Environmental Change Upon Behavior of Hospitalized Schizophrenic Patients, *Journal of Clinical Psychology, 24,* pp. 470-475, 1968.
14. D. L. DeVries, Effects of Environmental Change and of Participation on the Behavior of Mental Patients, *Journal of Consulting and Clinical Psychology, 32,* pp. 532-536, 1968.
15. A. Lipman, A Socio-Architectural View of Life Through Old People's Homes, *Gerontologia Clinica, 10,* pp. 88-101, 1968.
16. W. H. Ittelson, L. G. Rivlin and H. M. Proshansky, The Use of Behavioral Maps in Environmental Psychology, in H. M. Proshansky, W. H. Ittelson and L. G. Rivlin, (eds.), *Environmental Psychology,* Holt, Rinehart & Winston, New York, 1970.
17. E. B. Brody, (ed.), *Behavior in New Environments,* Sage, Beverly Hills, California, 1970.
18. T. S. Holmes and T. H. Holmes, Short-Term Intrusions Into the Life Style Routine, *Journal of Psychosomatic Research, 14,* pp. 121-132, 1970.
19. K. K. Schooler, The Effects of Changes in Residential Environment, *Proceedings of the Ninth International Congress of Gerontology,* Kiev, U.S.S.R., July, 1972.
20. R. J. Beck, S. B. Cohen, K. H. Craik, M. Dwyer, G. F. McCleary and S. Wapner, Studying Environmental Moves and Relocations, *Environment and Behavior, 5,* pp. 335-349, 1973.
21. M. P. Lawton, Ecology and Aging, in L. A. Pastalan and D. H. Carson, (eds.), *The Spatial Behavior of Older People,* University of Michigan, Institute of Gerontology, Ann Arbor, 1970.

part three

INSTITUTIONAL DILEMMAS

chapter 10

BODY IMAGE AND STAFF-TO-RESIDENT DEPORTMENT IN A HOME FOR THE AGED[1]

Wilbur H. Watson

How do the appearances of disability among the aged affect the conduct of nursing staff in nursing homes? In other words, are there any differences in staff conduct which vary systematically with appearances of disability in residents' behavior, for example, residents' dependencies on prosthetic devices for ambulation and recurrent "soiling" of the body and bedclothes as a result of incontinence. Is there a relationship between staff status differences and patterns of face-to-face interaction with residents? The problem of the relationship between social conduct, social status and images of the appearances of others is part of the larger problem of the relationship between social structure and interpersonal behavior. This paper presents the results of a series of exploratory observations of face-to-face interaction between nursing staff and residents in a home for the aged, and attempts an interpretation of those results. It was the intent to provide some insights toward answers to the foregoing questions and suggest some directions for future research into social interaction in homes for the aged.

[1] The study forming the basis of this report was made possible by USPHS grant No. 5-T01 HD 00186-03 for training in social gerontology, University of Pennsylvania, and the facilities of the Gerontological Research Center of Philadelphia, Pennsylvania. I am indebted to Dr.'s Otto Pollak, Erving Goffman and Robert Maxwell for helpful comment and criticism during the preparation of this paper.

In nursing homes, hospitals for the "mentally ill," and institutions for the severely retarded, custodial and "therapeutic" staff are daily confronted with resident-centered events which require their intervention—not infrequently resulting in direct or indirect physical contact with the residents. Common occasions for contact include those in which the custodial obligations of an aide or orderly may lead him to take part in cleansing the body of an incontinent resident (an example of direct contact). Instances of indirect contact include room-cleaning, bedcloth-changing or relocation of a resident in his wheelchair.

It is a truism that contact or touching relationships are necessary to the provision of care (whether custodial or therapeutic) to residents of a nursing home. However, it does not necessarily follow that the staff orientations toward residents will function in ways complementary to maintenance and rehabilitative programs of a home, for example, those intended to engender resident-to-resident (or resident-to-staff) interaction, resident self grooming, dressing, feeding, and other performances commonly associated with daily living activity (Brown 1964; Wright 1960, pp. 106–137).

In their study of a mental hospital (1954), Stanton and Schwartz found that at least some aspects of the disturbances of patients could be traced to the institutional structure. Included in hospital social structures are their medical and paramedical staff (that is, nurses, aids, orderlies, and so on). These staff members are not to be understood as a loose conglomerate of nursing personnel; instead, it can be established that these personnel usually form an orderly network of interacting members in whose social organization the residents (or patients) are integral participants (Stanton and Schwartz, 1954).

In the organization of health care programs, disruptive factors in attempts to establish networks of norms conducive to linking staff and residents in cooperative interaction do not simply result from one actor or a small group of actors failing to perform in a manner appropriate to formalized demands. Rather, disruptive and noncooperative conduct often develops from disparities between informal systems of valuations which, in addition to the formal value system (although not necessarily complementary to it), informs the different actors or groups in the selection of modes of conduct in a given social situation (Pace 1957, pp. 582–583).

Strides toward control of factors contributing to disruptive conduct can, in part, be achieved through greater insight into (1) patterns of situated conduct in environments intended for therapeutic purposes and (2) the valuational (or ideological) perspectives which influence actors' interpretations of symbolic objects, (for example, a debilitated body, or a nurse with a black or white face), and mediate encounters of actors who happen to be co-present to each other. The information gained through such research will be useful both to the sociology of institutions, and other complex organizations (particularly of health care facilities), and to agents of such organizations in planning programs for training direct care staff.

Given the apparent bearing of staff conduct and social organization on patient behavior, an important first step in the direction of further insight into situated conduct of staff is to determine the types of observable staff conduct that are manifest on occasions of staff-resident interaction. Insofar as types or styles of staff deportment are discernible, the next order of analysis is to determine their interrelationships and factors associated with variations in styles.

The purpose of this study was to ascertain the presence of types and variations in conduct of nursing personnel on occasions of staff-to-resident events in a Jewish home for the aged in a northeastern metropolis of the U.S. A staff-to-resident event was any occasion, for example, medicine passing, food serving, or grooming, in which a staff member entered into the immediate presence of a resident (that is, within touching distance by way of an extended arm) and ended when the staff member completed his task as symbolized by adducting his arms (that is, drawing them) to his body, pointing his face and body away from the resident, and walking away or orienting to another resident, staff member, or ward event.

An attempt was made through direct observation to determine what, if any, differences were manifest in staff touching and face-to-face conduct when a staff member had occasion to enter into the immediate presence of a resident. Secondly, in the analysis of the data collected, an attempt was made to determine whether the discernible styles and instances of touching and face-to-face conduct varied across staff-status levels and degree of resident disability. Finally, the variations in touching and face-to-face conduct were analyzed for their general implications for conduct in face-to-face situations.

STATEMENT OF METHODS

Setting

In addition to differences in personnel performances, for instance, nurses and nursing assistants, sharp distinctions between residents of the two floors (selected for this study) provided contextual phenomena against which to observe staff-to-resident events. These floors (*A* and *B*) were selected on the basis of differences between the aggregates of residents on a continuum of medically diagnosed brain damage and resident ability to perform (or manage) self-care in accordance with the normative demands of social situations on the floor.

Floor-*A* was occupied by 44 residents (5 male and 39 female) whose mean age was 84 years. The disabilities of the residents were such that most required assistance from nursing staff for accomplishing such daily routines as dressing, grooming, toileting, and feeding. Furthermore, resident engagement in verbal levels of interaction with staff was markedly absent. Perhaps the two most useful indicators of the degree of disability on this floor were (1) the prevalence of resident dependency on wheel chairs for ambulation beyond their bedrooms (ranging between 65-75 percent), and (2) the prevalence of anal and bladder incontinence, about 83 percent. While there was some variation among residents on Floor-*A* relative to abilities to perform roles without staff assistance, as a group the residents were comparatively more physically and socially disabled than any other aggregate of residents in the home.

Floor-*B* was occupied by 74 residents (10 male and 64 female) whose mean age was 83 years. The residents of Floor-*B*, in contrast to Floor-*A*, generally were able to ambulate themselves (with out the use of wheel chairs), although some did use walking canes or "walking cages." It was not unusual to observe Floor-*B* residents walking the full length of the corridor or using the elevators unassisted. Incontinence was rare (or less frequently reported) on Floor-*B*. Residents were generally able to dress, feed and toilet themselves. Furthermore, some residents participated in occupational rehabilitation and other programs operated within the context of the nursing home.

On the occasion of a staff-to-resident event on either floor, attention was focused through direct observation on the manner in which the staff member deported himself to the resident with particular reference to staff posture, physical distancing from the resident, gestures, and touching (or relative rendering of the staff's body to touch by) the resident.

To facilitate analyses of the data collected in this study, the nursing staff were classified according to (1) rank-order of responsibility relative to decision-making about managing a residential floor and (2) assignment to tasks (varying from custodial to paramedical) pertaining to the delivery of direct care services to residents of the home. Nurses (RN's and LPN's) were distinguished from nurses' aides and orderlies with the nurses considered as higher status staff on the dimensions of decision-making responsibility and task assigment. It was assumed that insofar as differences in social status are associated with self-images and valuations of others (Weber 1958, pp. 186–188, 190–191; Goffman 1963, pp. 126–139) a comparative analysis of status groups among nursing personnel could reveal important differences in patterns of deportments and implications of status group valuations of the residents served.

Against the background of distinctions in staff functioning and resident populations described above, a distinction between three styles of staff-to-resident deportment is presented.

Touching (or physical contact) is present in each of the three styles of staff-to-resident deportment. However, the orientation of the face of the staff member differs in each style. It is proposed here that insight into the meaning of the event of touching for the staff member can be gained, in part, (1) through the analysis of situated differences in orientations of staff faces, gestures and distancing during touching events, and (2) by analyses of the presentation (or absence) of ordinary gestures of deference, such as salutations, against the background of the status of the person touched (or the degree of the disability of the resident). The resident's bodily state may be symbolic of certain risks to befoulment or profanation of the staff member.

STYLES OF STAFF-TO-RESIDENT DEPORTMENT

One style of touching and face-orienting deportment (Type 1) was characterized by the staff member's entry into interaction with the resident by offering a greeting, for example, "good morning," or "how are you," while simultaneously orienting (or "pointing") his face to that of the resident. Not infrequently, verbal interaction accompanied this style, although not ordinarily for the duration of the touching event. While serving the resident, it was seldom the case that the staff member oriented his face or body away from the resident to engage in interaction with others situationally present. However, it was not unusual for him to glance briefly toward events occurring nearby. Generally, the orientation of the staff face—in this style of conduct—seemed to alternate primarily between a focus on that part of the resident's body being served and the resident's face. Having completed the care of the resident, the staff member would terminate the interaction process with a verbal "farewell," or a glance at the resident's face; or a smile and clasp of the resident's hands in his own, or some other gesture or combination of comments and gestures.

The second style (Type II) of touching and face-orienting conduct was characterized by a primary orientation of the staff member's face to that part of the resident's body being treated or served. Any kind of verbal exchange between staff and resident was the exception, rather the rule, in this style. It was common for no verbal interaction to take place, even insofar as greetings and farewells were concerned. The staff member, in this style, would occasionally glance away from the resident's body, but necessarily toward a situationally present activity. More frequently, the occasions for glancing away from the resident in this style were characterized by pointing the face to a wall or an area of the floor. Generally, the orientation of the staff face in this second style of deportment was to the point of touch and manipulation of the resident's body with some scanning of peripheral spaces.

Thirdly, there was a style of touching and face-orienting (Type III) in which the staff member's face (and occasionally his whole body) was pointed to an external behavioral event or a face engagement with another staff member while retaining a touching relationship with the resident. As in the second style of staff-to-resident conduct, verbal interaction with the resident was also uncommon, whether during the initiation, duration, or termination of the engagement. There were occasions when the staff member would glance for an instant at the face of the resident, especially during lulls in his preoccupations with external events. More commonly, however, attention to the resident was given to the part of the body being served, for instance, in cleaning legs or arms and combing hair.

Unlike either of the first two styles, it was characteristic in the latter style of deportment that the staff member would proceed through the treatment or service ritual, for example, taking a blood pressure reading or grooming, with marked dispatch. Finally, although the staff member in this style of deportment seemed eager to engage external (staff) others in interaction, greetings, farewells, and other kinds of deferential interchange were generally absent from the gestures that staff accorded the resident.

STAFF STATUS AND STYLES OF DEPORTMENT

The foregoing distinctions between styles of staff-to-resident deportment were based on an analysis of observations of staff-to-resident events without regard to differences in staff status. To recapitulate, the Type I style of deportment was characterized by staff initiation and termination of the interactive event via greetings and farewells, with verbal interaction and face-orienting staff conduct during the interim. The Type II style of deportment was characterized by entry into the interactive event by a relatively direct approach to, and focus on, the part of the resident's body to be served. In addition, staff conduct was characterized by an absence of salutations at the initiation and termination of interactive events with little or no verbal interaction or face-orienting to the resident during the interim. Finally, the Type III style of deportment was characterized in general by an absence of verbal interaction between staff and resident although it was not unusual to observe the same staff person intermittently engaged in verbal interaction with another staff member who was situationally present during the servicing of the resident.

Given these distinctions between styles of staff-to-resident deportment, attention was then turned to the extent to which styles varied when staff were compared relative to status differences.

Secondly (in this section) attention is given to the following question: When status differences are held constant and resident disability is varied, to what extent are differences manifest in styles of staff-to-resident deportment?

Since styles of deportment did not vary markedly within status levels, except in association with variations in degree of resident disability, it may be useful—at the outset—to briefly recapitulate the distinctions between the aggregates of residents on the two floors. The floors were distinguished primarily by degrees of medically diagnosed brain damage and self-care abilities of the residents. Although there were other floors available for observation, the two used in this study were deliberately selected as approximations to polar types on a continuum of resident disability. In as much as degree and kind of resident disability may influence styles of staff-to-resident deportment, the situations on residential floors within and between which staff conduct was observed had to be clearly distinguished by degrees of disability. Finally, it was assumed that the task assignments of different staff members, for example, orderlies, aides, LPN's and RN's, were relatively homogeneous across particular wards. As such, despite the fact that observations were made on two different wards and specific staff persons did not have an equal nor randomly selected number of assignments on each of the two wards, observations were made in terms of units of staff-to-resident events, rather than in terms of specific persons. As described earlier in the methodology, the two areas of situated conduct will be referred to as Floor-*A* (extremely disabled) and Floor-*B* (least disabled).

In general, staff-to-resident touching and face-orienting conduct appeared to be more prevalent the lower the staff-status level on Floor-*A*. While it may be expected that, institutionally, orderlies and nurses' aides would be more likely than upper status personnel to perform such duties as assisting in grooming, feeding and dressing residents, it is not institutionally requisite that lower-status personnel orient themselves to face-to-face contact with residents when assisting them in these performances.

In general, lower-status nursing personnel (that is, orderlies and nurses' aides) on Floor-*A* were characterized by the Type I style of deportment as described above. In contrast, upper-status personnel were characterized by what may be referred to as Type III styles of deportment.

Not infrequently, an upper-status staff member would have occasion to initiate contact and care for a resident on Floor-*A*, but almost invariably would thereafter call in a lower-order-staff member to complete the task.

The instances of Type II styles of deportment did not permit a distinction between upper and lower status personnel on Floor-*A*. Instead, this style of deportment was as often characteristic of personnel in the upper-status levels as of members of the lower-status levels on Floor-*A*.

Up to this point, it may be suggested that the description of staff deportment and differences in distribution of styles on Floor-*A* is no more than what would be expected of nursing staff within the context of a nursing home. However, the variations in styles of deportment on Floor-*A* by status level of personnel are not the same as on Floor-*B*.

On Floor-*B*, staff-to-resident touching and face-orienting conduct seemed to appear more often the higher the staff-status level. As such, upper-status personnel (that is, LPN's and RN's) were generally characterized by a Type I style of deportment (in contrast to Type III as the model category for upper-status personnel on Floor-*A*). Furthermore, lower status staff on Floor-*B* (in contrast to Floor-*A*) were characterized by both Types II and III styles of deportment in orienting to residents.

In general then, what, on Floor-*A*, appeared to be an institutionally determined relationship between lower-status nursing staff positions and frequent instances of touch and face-to-face interaction with residents, was not supported by the observations on Floor-*B*. On Floor-*B*, the obverse proposition was suggested by the data. Insofar as the preliminary observations on which this report is based are (to some extent) reflective of more than random variation in styles of staff-to-resident deportment between Floors *A* and *B*, one question which suggests itself is: What would contribute to an explanation of the variations in staff-to-resident conduct by degree of resident disability, if not the formal occupational structure of the nursing home?

BODY IMAGE, STAFF STATUS AND STYLES OF DEPORTMENT

Whatever may be the images and sentiments (sacred or profane) that others attribute to the body of a particular person or group of persons, it is proposed that an actor who is at any given time located within the context of a particular gathering that has conveyed to him images of what it considers proper conduct may, nevertheless, hold private images of himself which are counter to the public images and sentiments of him (Goffman, 1963, pp. 8-11, 66-72). As such, and insofar as self-other images influence styles of staff-to-resident deportment, it may be anticipated that styles of deportment will be manifest which, while not being fully articulated with the formal structure of a social situation, for instance, the demands for a "therapeutic milieu" within a nursing home, may, nevertheless, be intricately tied in with situated conduct through informal normative codes.

Taking the body as a point of reference, and given the proposition that every individual manifests some demands for personal territorial rights (Lyman and Scott 1967, pp. 244–246; Goffman 1961, p. 243),[2] we can begin to probe for insights into the phenomenon whereby particular appearances of the bodies of others, for example, amputated, paralyzed or incontinent aged—while designated by some able-bodied individuals as profane and potentially befouling should they be touched—may be regarded as noncontaminating by others. When an individual or group is the object of negative (or discrediting) public sentiment but, nevertheless retains and shares with particular others positive (or compensatory) sentiments about certain self-attributes, for example, being an ex-convict or visibly deformed, this intragroup structure of sentiments may function as a "shield" or "buffer" against the otherwise deleterious effects of "degradation ceremonies" performed by others (Garfinkel 1956, p. 420; Durkheim 1951, pp. 297–325). It is against the background of differences in symbolic

[2] Personal territory is conceived as that space, including the body surface and sub-surface areas, over which an individual manifests a "private claim, and . . . develops some comforts, control, and tacit rights that he shares with no other individual except by his invitation." Conduct, such as recurrently adjusting physical distances between self and others, alternating postural stances and other manners of deportment may be read as markers of the boundary and accessibility of personal territory.

media through which the body is viewed and structures of sentiment pertaining to its deportment, state of health, and its uses and abuses, that the differences in styles of staff-to-resident deportment will be discussed in this section.

If the residents from Floors *A* and *B* were grouped and rank ordered relative to degree of functionability and socially approved manners of deportment, the Ward-*A* residents would come to occupy most of the bottom and lower-middle status positions. If, similarly, the nursing staff from each ward were grouped and rank-ordered—by extent of functionability relative to caretaking and socially approved deportment—the orderlies and nurses' aides would probably be distributed in a fashion not unlike that of the Floor-*A* residents in a structure of statuses including all residents.

Now, whether as a result of shared sentiments about self-other images arising from formal institutional requirements and experiences shared through being in similar status positions; or, as a result of institutional constraints bearing on the limits to which any given actor or group may affiliate with others, it may be expected that lower-status nursing personnel will move into and out of touching relationships with the more disabled residents (in Ward-*A*) more frequently and with less restraint than upper-status personnel. In addition to occupying a status level within the nursing staff similar to that of the Ward-*A* residents (when all residents are combined), both sets of these lower level persons (orderlies and aides, and extremely disabled residents) may be considered as the relatively profane in their particular groups. As such, the risk of befoulment of self by touching the body of another like-self (that is, similarly labeled as contaminating or not-contaminating), may be viewed by the staff member (whether low or high status) as a less risk to self befoulment (or self-negation) than when the state of the resident's body and public image is the opposite of that of the staff member.

That self-other differences relative to the distribution of visible and degrading bodily attributes may have a bearing on styles of staff-to-resident deportment is suggested in Goffman's discussion of mixed contacts between the " 'visibly' stigmatized" and "normals." He suggests that ". . . the stigmatized individual—at least the 'visibly' stigmatized one—will have special reasons for feeling that mixed social situations make for anxious unanchored interaction. But if this is so, then it is to be suspected that we normals will find these situations shaky too." (Goffman, 1963, p. 18).

Unlike mixed contacts, it may be expected that when a staff member (who has images of his body as being uncontaminated) enters into the presence of an able bodied resident who is (or is publicly imagined to be) in a similarly sacred physical state, each will probably find the others presence ratifying to his self image (that is, confirmation by non-negation) at least in regard to body image. On the other hand, what happens when a person (for example, of upper staff status) who, although deporting himself so as to suggest a comparatively sacred (or non-touchable) state of his body—enters into the immediate presence of an extremely disabled resident (symbolically profane compared to the upper status staff)? His style of deportment should be expected to exhibit noticeable restraint enabling avoidance of the risk of befouling himself through touching the resident (e.g., in giving treatment) or in being befouled should the extremely disabled resident successfully reach out and touch him. Patterned avoidance of contact with residents (or minimizing such contract) may be symbolic of a staff member's predilection to avoid befoulment of a resident as when a lower status staff member comes into the presence of an able bodied resident or when black staff members of certain persuasions come into the presence of a white able bodied resident or staff member. Befoulment, in this sense, may be thought of as the resultant transformation in (or of) the symbolic state of a sacred body (or other object) resulting from its contact or association with that which is its moral negation (that is, that which must not be actually becomes associated, or in-touch, with the object).

Illustrative of the deportment of some upper-status nursing staff when in the immediate presence of extremely disabled residents is the following event observed on Floor-*A*:

> A nurse (RN) while walking down the ward corridor was stopped by a resident who had reached out to grasp the nurse's arm. While holding the nurse's arm, the resident pulled herself in close to the nurse so as to whisper something in the nurse's ear. At the same time, the nurse stiffened and drew her head to the side and backward with the effect of avoiding cheek-to-cheek contact with the resident.

This event suggests that the arm (or a clothed arm) is dispensable for contact with a potentially befouling person, but not the face. That different parts of the body may be differently valuated relative to risk of self befoulment is further implied by the fact that the same nurse (and others of upper-status) when in the presence of other nurses and on Floor-*B* were not infrequently observed to touch residents with no noticeable restraint in the process.

In contrast to the conduct of upper-status personnel on Floor-*A*, lower-status staff were more commonly characterized by the following conduct while moving about the ward corridor:

> Given a series of passings, orderlies have been observed to acknowledge the gesture of the extended arm and hand to the point of touching at the interfaces of his and the resident's fingertips or to clasp the outstretched hand of the resident. Nurse-aides have also been observed to acknowledge patient gestures to them. But unlike orderlies, nurse-aides seemed to engage less often in touching conduct (except when passing food trays, assisting with treatments, and toileting and dressing) while passing through the ward than in turnings-of-the-head to glance at, and occasionally to smile to or verbally greet, the resident.

All manners of deportment characteristic of lower level personnel on Floor-*A* were, as indicated earlier, more characteristic of upper-status personnel on Floor-*B*. Although it may be unusual to consider befoulment processes from the point of view of the person who comes in contact with his status superior and who becomes subject to the risk of transgressing the boundaries of the territory of his status superior by himself or other-initiated interaction, the appropriateness of such an analysis follows from the proposed relationships between personal territory, the sacred, and befoulment processes as developed in this paper. In the analysis of the process by which one person selects another and proceeds to engage in face-to-face interaction, it is clearly important to consider status differences between the interactants. In addition, attention must be given to the systems of public images and the structures of those sentiments which shape each actor's private images and which are functionally related to his styles of self-to-other deportment.

CONCLUSIONS

The normative structure of a nursing home—particularly as regards actual nursing care—leads functionally into many occasions for staff-resident touching and face engagements, for example, in grooming, dressing, feeding and providing medicines and treatments. Concurrently, insofar as a staff member happens to be in-touch with a resident at any given moment, he is simultaneously situated in a way that is ecologically conducive to face-to-face interaction, although such interaction (or even talk) may not take place. However, it does not follow that in the absence of face engagements and talk there is no interaction.

In the foregoing report of a study of staff-to-resident deportment in a home for the aged, analysis of the data collected through direct observation yielded three patterns of interaction process in each of which considerable nonverbal idiom were manifest. Nonconscious patterning of conduct in situations of face-to-face interaction renders the observable patterns of conduct inaccessible to immediate control by the co-participants (Hall 1963, pp. 1003–1004). In addition, the absence of a "vocabulary of nonverbal idiom"—that is, unavailable to members of nursing home staff who are ordinarily charged with establishing "therapeutic environments"—is fundamental to the likelihood that non-talk content in the patterning of interaction will escape attention of supervisory personnel (and others) and remain largely out of programatic planning.

The practical importance of these considerations was suggested in the introductory section of this paper. It was proposed that, on occasion, nursing staff orientations to residents of a home may or may not function in ways complementary to programs intended for therapeutic purposes. To the extent that patterns of interaction process are taking place at levels which escape the attention of agents of therapeutic programs, a part of whose approach includes some type of in-service training for staff, it would behoove the agents of such programs to become more aware of their appearances as media (in face-to-face interaction) and other kinds of nonverbal idiom, for example, physical gestures and emotional expressions, particularly as they affect encounters with residents.

In addition to further research into nonverbal idiom in staff-to-resident interaction, it would be worthwhile to seek insights into the patterning of body idiom in staff-to-staff encounters, for instance, as between staff of similar and different statuses, sex, age, variations in appearances of blackness and whiteness, and other factors. As other studies have indicated (Stanton and Schwartz 1954; pp. 5–20; Pace 1957), a lack of consensus about what constitutes proper organization for social situations intended to facilitate therapeutic changes may subsequently be manifest in disparate modes of conduct among staff whose stated aims in relation to disabled others are presumably the same. Methodologically, valuational differences pertaining to the provision of care may be hidden from observers through staff control of occasions for talk, including selection of content and talking partners. However, given a vocabulary of body idiom, valuational differences may inadvertently seep through and become available for direct observation in the daily rounds of staff and residents who are recurrently entering into and passing out of situated face and touching engagements with each other.

REFERENCES

Brown, Florence L. 1964. Knowledge of body-image and nursing care of the patient with limb amputation. *J. psychiatric Nursing*, 397–410.

Durkheim, E. 1951. *Suicide*. Glencoe: The Free Press.

Garfinkel, H. 1956. Conditions of successful degradation ceremonies. *Amer. J. Soc.*, 61, 420–24.

Goffman, E. 1961. *Asylums*. New York: Anchor Books.

———. 1963. *Stigma*. Englewood Cliffs, N.J.: Prentice-Hall.

———. 1963. The neglected situation. *Amer. Anthropol.*, 66, 6, 1133–36.

Lyman, S. M., & Scott, M. B. 1967. Territoriality: A neglected sociological dimension. *Soc. Prob*. 15, 2, 244–46.

Pace, R. E. 1957. Situational therapy. *J. Personal.*, 25, 578–88.

Sommer, R. 1969. *Personal space*. Englewood Cliffs, N.J.: Prentice-Hall.

Stanton, A. H., & Schwartz, M. S. 1954. *The mental hospital*. New York: Basic Books.

Weber, M. 1958. *From Max Weber: Essays in sociology*, ed. H. H. Garth & C. Wright Mills. New York: Oxford Univ. Press.

Wright, B. 1960. *Physical disability: A psychological approach*. New York: Harper & Row.

chapter 11

NOTES ON THE NEGATIVE IMPLICATIONS OF BEING COMPETENT IN A HOME FOR THE AGED

Judith Posner

Current studies conducted from the ethnomethodological research perspective have emphasized the notion of *bona fide collectivity members*, a phrase adapted from Parsons. These sociologists use the term competence to refer to:

> . . . the claim that a collectivity member is entitled to exercise that he is capable of managing his everyday affairs without interference. That members take such claims for granted I refer to by speaking of a person as a "bona-fide" collectivity member [1].

This concept of bona fide collectivity membership suggests that underlying all social interaction are certain taken-for-granted assumptions, or tacit knowledge regarding what is "normal," "average" or "typical" behavior. In fact, this notion is quite similar to Goffman's delineation of a "stigma-less" person, i.e., wasp, middle-class, male, etc. [2]. It is therefore understandable that social phenomenologists are especially concerned with research into the nature of deviancy and members' labelling strategies, which give insight into what is normal, by focusing on members' constructions of what is abnormal, immoral or stigmatic [3].

The phenomenological perspective suggests that members implicitly presume that other members are normal, until proven otherwise, i.e., until they "give off" something or "give themselves away" by exhibiting their negative statuses. The purpose of the following paper will be to investigate a reversal of this ordinary members' method, a process which could be referred to as "innocent until proven guilty," by focusing on professional people processors' perceptions of residents in a Home for the Aged.

It will be contended that the particular inmate community at hand is pre-defined by members (both staff and inmates) as old, incompetent and abnormal. This fact of the perceptual frame of reference for viewing Geriatric residents, places them in a context which is the mirror image of normal social reality. What is normal for adult members becomes abnormal, unexpected behavior for old people, and *vice versa*. In short the game has changed, the tables have turned and definitions of winning and losing are totally reversed.

Parsons has defined the "sick role" in the context of a discussion of deviancy. He states that

> Illness is predominantly a withdrawal into a dependent relation. It is asking to be taken care of. It uses disability as the legitimization of this claim [4].

Thus, it may be fair to assume that persons who admit to a deviancy or abnormality, as evidenced in voluntary commitment to mental hospitals and old age Homes are making the sort of statement about themselves to which Parson alludes. Playing the sick role, like playing the deviant role, suggests that members are requesting other members to view them in terms of their "extenuating circumstances" or new rules of a new game. To present oneself as sick or deviant is to say to others that "I-am-not-to-be-judged-against-so-called-normals or so-called-normal-rules-of-the-game," which evaluates persons on the basis of competency or bona fide collectivity membership. Rather, it permits redefinition of one's evaluative and perceptual context. Thus, dichotomies like homosexuality vs. heterosexuality, old vs. young and male vs. female suggest that these ideal types live in different worlds, and they are perceived by others accordingly. We can therefore speak of sexually adjusted homosexuals, competent older people, and mature children without fear of contradiction. These do not reflect anomalies, but rather they reflect the fact that for a child–one can be mature, for a homosexual–one can be fairly adjusted, and for an older person–one can be relatively competent.

Anselm Strauss has suggested that therapy problems are membership problems [5]. He looks upon the process of therapy as a sort of status passage rite, or identity transformation ritual. Similarly, entrance into the Home may be regarded as a crisis rite for old people, who are at such a time publicly and officially acknowledging their incompetence and dependence on others, or their withdrawal into the "sick" role. Thus, entrance into the institution represents a statement about self as well as reflecting the general public's social perception of old people, which signifies the end of one game (normal society or the *outside*) and the beginning of another (total institution or the *inside*).

THE CENTER

At the present time the Geriatric Center under investigation consists of three distinct institutions with the following approximate capacities for service:

Home for the Aged	426
Senior Citizens Day Care Center	350 participants a week
Geriatric Hospital	160

This complex is designed to give total care for the aged and chronically ill under one umbrella administration. Future plans include an expansion of this continuity of services including, for example, senior citizens apartments and other less structured social settings. In essence, then, services represent responses to varying degrees of mental and physical incompetence,[1] a continuum of clients' incompetences.

Admission into the Home (Hospital or Day Care) is awarded to those who are perceived by staff, primarily social case workers, to *need* the Center environment most. Before any individual is admitted into the Home it is presumed that

> Every effort was made to help the aged person manage outside the Home, and only when the Home felt that every effort had been made was an individual given priority for admission.
>
> Our policy of keeping people out until they can no longer function in the community is sound, however it does mean people are often admitted in a more deteriorated condition. (From Home literature.)

Thus, the Home is always viewed as a court of last resort. Social workers recognize that institutionalization of any sort is only to be employed as a lesser of alternative evils. Similarly, the Day Care program is employed as a particular sort of preventative measure, which will hopefully help elderly persons to maintain themselves in the community on their own for as long as possible. Because of this fact, case reports which are presented at admission committee meetings are oriented toward documenting the reasons why clients must be admitted into the Home. By way of analogy, just as lawyers argue for the innocence of their clients, social workers are placed in the situation of proving beyond a shadow of a doubt that their clients are indeed guilty, i.e., they are stigmatized, incompetent or incapable of functioning on their own. In short, social workers must prove that their clients are *not* bona fide collectivity members!

> At present the medical staff feel that further strain or pressure would put this brittle woman in a *precarious position*. We are therefore presenting her application for approval at this time. (From case report of 88 year old woman.)

[1] However, Center literature does point out that there is no point in admitting "hopelessly senile" persons into their institution, as most facilities there would be wasted on them. Therefore such persons are encouraged to go to a less elaborate Nursing Home.

To be granted admission into the Home may be advantageous in many respects, and most clients are eager for their final approval for admission after months spent on long waiting lists. But clearly, the implications of "winning" admission have unintended consequences which confuse the criteria for evaluating social behavior within the institution's confines. With regard to normal society and bona fide membership rules, winning admission means leaving one social reality for another and changing games, rules and players.

THE HOME: A MIRROR IMAGE OF THE WORLD OUTSIDE

As stated, the common-sense assumption underlying Home social life, i.e., residents are old and incompetent, is the antithesis of the common-sense assumption operating in most normal social life, on the outside.

> The interpretive scheme of the total institution automatically begins to operate as soon as the inmate enters, the staff having the notion that entrance is *prima facie* evidence that one must be the kind of person the institution was set up to handle. A man in a political prison must be traitorous; a man in a prison must be a lawbreaker; a man in a mental hospital must be sick. If not traitorous, criminal or sick, why else would he be there [6].

The implications of this fact are infinite and all-pervasive. Behavior usually thought to be surprising, or abnormal for normal, competent adult members will be expected, or implicitly defined, as normal for elderly Home residents. It has been stated that the primary purpose of the Home is to shelter and take care of incompetent elderly persons. Therefore all administrative efforts are ostensibly in this direction. Thus, those who are most incompetent can take best advantage of Home services and facilities. In essence, the Home is oriented toward the *least competent*. Although typically, one tends to think of the advantages of competency, one of the most significant structural features of Home life is the way in which being a bona fide collectivity member can work against inmates, as the normal social expectations there are the reverse of those normally presumed. They are therefore unexpected, unprepared for and inappropriate. In addition to the fact that those who are most incompetent gain access into the Home, these individuals are also offered the most attention when they arrive. The following is an attempt to document how perceptions of incompetence at the Home structure social relations, in a reverse manner from ordinary society.

Upon walking through the Home, it is observed for example, that single rooms are far more prevalent on Special Care floors than on either Standard or Nursing Care floors. (Note: the Home is divided into 3 subsections respectively, Special Care (floors 3 and 4) Standard Care (floors 5, 6 and 7) and Nursing Care (floors 8, 9 and 10). The senile, or the most mentally and physically incompetent members of the Home, are allowed the luxury of privacy more frequently than more competent residents. This is particularly intriguing since some of the Special Care residents may not even be aware of the difference between being in private or public. One might assume, and rightly so, that the reason for this difference in single room availability is not so much an effort to cater to the residents' actual desires,[2] but rather due to the fact that residents in this competence category exhibit so much peculiar or idiosyncratic behavior that it is functionally impractical, from an administrative standpoint, to room such persons together. It is assumed that rooming quasi-senile residents together would result in even further noise and chaos on these floors. Thus, these residents' mental incompetences and social isolation from others is reflected in their private rooms symbolizing their private worlds. And the scarce contents of their rooms further reflects their social isolation, i.e., there is a striking lack of personal acquisitions such as family photos and personal knick-knacks on Special Care floors.

Similarly, on Nursing and Standard Care, it appears that residents who have the most severe problems in the areas of mental and physical incompetences, making it difficult for them to get along with others, are usually afforded a private room. The reasons for this are obvious enough. Because single rooms are in low supply as they are more expensive to maintain than doubles,[3] it is more efficient, from an administrative standpoint, to move those residents who are the most difficult to get along with, rather than those who cannot get along with them. An example of such a situation was related to me by an informant:

> Mrs. K. (Standard Care) complained bitterly about her roommate who had bladder problems, causing occasional messes. She requested a room change but was told it was impossible at the time. The situation continued to get worse, and Mrs. K. says she often cleaned up the messes herself, as the nurse or housekeeper took too long to get there. She continued, though disgruntled, to live with the situation until a single room became available. At that time, and to her surprise, her incompetent roommate was assigned to the new room and Mrs. K. received another roommate with whom she is presently living. When Mrs. K. related this story to me, she commented on the irony of the fact that the "other lady" got the single room, for which she had been anxiously waiting.

Another incident suggests this theme, as it relates to emotional and/or mental competence.

> A resident, Mrs. S. (Standard Care) and several other women were seated together when a social worker approached the group and began to discuss the coming Home fashion show. She asked the ladies if they would like to assist by being models.

The fashion show is clearly one of the highlights of the year for female residents. The women always appear very thrilled to participate in such an event, and they usually get their hair set by the Beauty Salon, wear corsages and also have their pictures taken by professional photographers. All in all, it appears as though this particular program is a sort of last chance to be the "belle of the ball." Residents act with coyness and girlish pride as they parade on and off the stage. Staff too, tend to see this activity in a similar light. In fact, some staff who are involved in

[2] This may be a questionable assumption, however, as pointed out by Lawton and Bader: "Wish for privacy by Young and Old," in *J. of Gerontology*, Vol. 25, no. 1.

[3] Families do pay extra for single rooms if they can afford it. However, even if they pay in full, this does not cover the actual incremental costs involved.

choosing the ladies to model the outfits, appear to make their judgements on the basis of who needs the ego-lift or morale-boost most. It takes little intellectual capacity and/or physical competence to participate in this show, which consists of walking or wheeling around for a few moments. Wheelchair residents often participate in this program by modelling housecoats, robes and other applicable items. Thus there is the suggestion that individuals are chosen to participate on the basis of the *un*attractiveness and *in*competence, and this runs clearly contrary to our usual expectations about fashion models on the "outside." After watching several of these shows I cannot emphasize strongly enough the elements of self-esteem that are involved here, and the effect that being a model has on the women. Therefore, when the social worker approached the particular group at hand, Mrs. S. spoke up and inquired if she, too, could be a model.

> The social worker said "yes," and that was that. Mrs. S. was very excited and proceeded to tell her family of the coming event. A week or so later, however, when the social worker came around again, relating the details of the show, Mrs. S. asked what she was going to wear in the show. The social worker responded that she had reconsidered the matter and she didn't feel Mrs. S. *needed* to be a model after all.

The underlying assumptions which probably brought the social worker to such a conclusion are obvious enough. Mrs. S. has many interests in the Home, including participation in the more "high-level functioning programs" such as the Women's Discussion Group and the Resident Council. In addition, she is entertained outside the Home quite regularly by family and friends. Except for her recent stroke, from which she is "recovering beautifully," she has few ailments "for a woman her age." She is sometimes forgetful and confused, but her generally perceived "high intelligence" appears to more than compensate for this failing. In sum, Mrs. S. is looked upon by staff and residents alike as one of the resident elite, or one of the most generally competent people in the Home. This perception and social labelling probably leads the social worker to conclude that such a woman does not need the opportunity of proving herself as a model as much as other residents who are not capable of doing anything else. The fact that Mrs. S. felt that she needed to be a model, then was not taken into account. As Mrs. S. related this incident to me, some time after its occurrence, she commented that she had "had it" with all the social workers. She stated that from the time that she first entered the Home they have done nothing for her. Before admission they "laid out the red carpet," and treated her with respect and great attentiveness, but ever since then she feels that she has been ignored.

> When you come here the first time they make a big fuss over you, but once you are settled they don't pay any attention to you. Social workers are *superfluous*.

In conclusion, the implications of these anecdotes are clear. Some residents in the Home who are viewed as relatively competent and unproblematic are pretty well left on their own after admission. This and other similar features of Home life are peculiarly contradictory to the fact that entrance into the Home is based on the labelling of "incompetent" which residents must have more or less acknowledged when they were admitted. In essence, the loss in status which accompanies entrance into the Home may not even be compensated for with the profuse aid and attention expected by many residents. For example, recently in Day Care a new division of labor amongst the case social workers has been instituted. Some social workers are responsible for processing people into the Day Care. Others watch over residents after admission. However, only those residents who are problematic are assigned to two sets of social workers. Competent Day Care members are only assigned to group workers after admission and have no individual case workers. In other words, the withdrawal into the sick role is only half-acknowledged here. Thus, it is not surprising that there is much confusion at the Home over staff/inmate role expectations, based on the perception of mental and physical capabilities and its relevance for the structuring of social interaction.

If we return momentarily to the analogy of the game, and the notion of changing games, rules and players, the above ethnographic examples may be interpreted from the perspective of an exchange model based on Parson's statement. The sick or deviant person legitimates his dependence on others by admitting to his incompetence. The elderly person is normally seen to have done this when he enters the Home. Here he even takes on a new form of address, that is he becomes a "resident," which while not so stigmatizing a term as "inmate," has many of its connotations. As Parson implies, the resident now accepts this stigmatized or low-status label because of its side benefits or "payoffs." With regard to the Home, the payoff is being treated as a certain kind of special person with special privileges. But clearly, specialness is a relative concept, and there are more special persons to be processed in the Home and other institutions for the incompetent than there are special persons processors. In addition, the Home literature espouses the official philosophy that residents should not perceive themselves as incompetent and dying just because they have entered an Old Folks Home.

> . . . the older person will walk into the institution head upright, knowing what he is doing to the extent that he is capable of knowing it. . . . It means we should expect him to walk in, choosing to live there and not to die there. . . . It means being ready, aye ready, to tell him that there are plenty of holes in this world he can find to crawl into if he wished only for a place to die . . . It means expecting him to be helpful up to his capacity . . .

Thus, a factor in the analysis of social interaction and people processing in the Home is the official community and institutional philosophy of rehabilitative therapy, which addresses itself to the notion that entrance into an Old Folks Home can signify a positive phase in identity transformation, contrary to the negative moral career of the inmate as delineated by Goffman. In fact, many residents in the Home are perceived by staff as developing new interests in life after institutional admission. Thus, borrowing the terminology from Van Gennep's classic study of crisis rites [7] it may be contended that the Home focuses on the incorporation stage, rather than the separation stage emphasized by Goffman's perspective. However, it should also be acknowledged that there is something vaguely ironic about the fact that rehabilitation therapy is administered to geriatric patients who are clearly acknowledged as members who have entered into the inevitable final status passage of dying. In fact, residents seldom if ever leave a Home for the Aged by any other means than death.

In conclusion, the Home under investigation operates on the basis of the two contradictory cultural themes described. On the one hand, residents in a Home for the Aged are pre-defined as incompetent, and must demonstrate their incompetence in order to gain admission into the Home and be afforded attention there. On the other hand, official rehabilitative philosophy discourages staff from treating residents as incompetent invalids. Because the commodity of aid and attention is in higher demand than its supply, residents may be seen to vie for its distribution. Similarly, staff who are in the position of distributing privileges do so on the basis of implicit rehabilitative philosophy which suggests 1) don't help the resident unless he really needs it and 2) help those who need aid most, first. Thus, residents like Mrs. K. and Mrs. S., who represent the "cream of the crop" have not really exchanged one game for another, as initially suggested, but rather they are playing two games at once, or better still, they live in a state of "gamelessness" in which rules from both worlds are operating simultaneously. That is, they are deemed *incompetent enough* to lose in the external community, and they are forced to leave it, but they are, in a very real sense, *too competent* to win the game on the inside. Bringing this analogy to its absurd conclusion, relatively competent inmates in an institution such as the one described (or any other institution catering to incompetents) sometimes reflect the classic, contemporary theme of Catch 22, i.e., no matter what they do, they lose.

REFERENCES

1. Garfinkel, H. *Studies in Ethnomethodology*, Prentice-Hall, 1967, p. 57.
2. Goffman, E. *Stigma*, Prentice-Hall, 1963, p. 128.
3. An unpublished paper by M. Petrunik and C. D. Shearing traces, in an historical fashion, *Normative and Pehnomenological Approaches to the Study of Deviancy*. Jack Douglas suggests a similar thesis in the preface to *Deviance and Respectability*, Basic Books, 1970.
4. Parsons, T. *The Social System*, 1951, p. 285.
5. Strauss, A. "Transformations of Identity" in A. Rose (ed.) *Human Behavior and Social Processes*, Houghton Mifflin, 1962.
6. Goffman, E. *Asylums*, Anchor Books, 1961, p. 84.
7. Van Gennep, A. *The Rites of Passage*. Translated by Monika Vizedom and Gabrielle Caffee, University of Chicago Press, 1960.

chapter 12

GAME-ANALYZABLE DILEMMAS IN A RETIREMENT VILLAGE: A CASE STUDY[1]

Victor W. Marshall

Retirement communities are a relatively recent and rapidly growing alternative for the aging individual as he decides what kind of living arrangement will best provide the security and supports he might need for his last years. A feature of many such facilities is the provision of a "life-care" contract which guarantees lifetime residency in the community, including care in an affiliated or attached extended care facility should this become necessary. In the "life-care" arrangement the resident typically pays a substantial entrance fee, and signs a contract which commits him to pay monthly rental or maintenance fees for the duration of his life. From the perspective of the owners and administrators of such communities, the entrance fees can be applied to the amortization of the mortgage on the physical plant, while the monthly rental payments can be utilized to cover operating expenses. In this paper I will describe this situation as one of conflict of interest between the administration and the residents, drawing on game theory to elucidate a particular case and suggest its wider applicability.

[1] This paper was presented at the 25th Annual Meeting of the Gerontological Society, San Juan, Puerto Rico, December 20, 1972, and expands some considerations raised in the author's doctoral dissertation. The assistance of The Canada Council, Princeton University, the residents and administration of Glen Brae is greatfully acknowledged.

Additionally, I hope to demonstrate the value of a game-theoretical approach to some other issues relating to gerontology.

Game theory may be defined (Rapoport, 1959) as

> . . . an attempt to bring within the fold of rigorous deductive method those aspects of human behavior in which conflict and cooperation are conducted in the context of choices among alternatives whose range of outcomes is known to the fullest extent by the participants.

My own use of game theory is non-mathematical, but involves the following assumptions which are common to all game theories:

1. Participants (or "players") in a game formulation are viewed as seeking to maximize utility (the excess of rewards over costs), or at least to "satisfice," or gain a quantity of rewards satisfactory enough to make playing the game worthwhile (Simon, 1957; American Behavioral Scientist, 1964).
2. Each player knows the preference patterns or preferred strategies of the other player. "Awareness that other social actors have goals, and a varied but finite set of means through which to realize them, constitutes the primary prerequisite for game action" (Lyman and Scott, 1970:31).
3. Each player is fully informed of the rewards and costs of alternative lines of action both for himself and for other players (American Behavioral Scientist, 1964; Rapoport, 1960:10).

Game-theoretical analysis attempts to construct a model of decision-making under the above conditions. The emphasis is on players basing their decision strategies on not only their own conception of goals and the means to their realization, but also on a complete knowledge of the perspective of the other player. That is, interaction is viewed as *strategic*, as a ". . . cycle of two players taking into consideration their consideration of each other's consideration, and so forth" (Goffman, 1970:137; *see also* Moore and Anderson, 1963). As most game theorists themselves admit (Luce and Raiffa, 1957:10; Ofshe and Ofshe, 1970:2; Boguslaw, 1965:56-58), the above conditions, which constitute a definition of "pure rationality," seldom if ever obtain in the real world, if only because the human mind does not have the information-processing capacities required (March and Simon, 1958:139; Simon, 1957:198). Nonetheless, human beings or players are generally recognized as intending to act rationally (Simon, 1957:199) even if they must act practically on the basis of incomplete knowledge of the situation at present and at some future time (Schutz, 1953). While a game-theoretical analysis can never give us an accurate picture of the real world, it can, then sensitize the observer to departures from pure rationality and their causes, especially as these involve the interplay between two or more persons each with limited knowledge and each making assumptions about the other, neither of which may be highly accurate.

It is possible, then, to use real data to see whether they fit the implications of a game-theory model (Morgan, 1963). My real data come from observation, interviewing, and documents gathered in a life-care retirement community I will call Glen Brae (Marshall, 1972), where approximately 400 residents have paid entrance fees ranging between $14,500 and $45,000, and committed themselves to a contract specifying monthly maintenance fees upwards of $330 for the rest of their lives, ". . . or such larger or smaller amount per month as may from time to time be determined to be necessary by the Corporation" (statement appearing in the Contract). The entrance fee is lost on a 2% monthly calculation such that any resident desiring to leave the community after fifty months, or dying at any time, will have lost his entire investment.

Because of the initial high payment, a move to Glen Brae would not be a good investment should the person not live very long; he might well find better ways to spend his money. On the other hand, because monthly payments extend for the duration of his life, the move to Glen Brae will not be a good investment should the person live too long and run out of money. A rational decision to enter Glen Brae thus depends fundamentally on an accurate prediction of life-expectancy, and secondly on an accurate estimate of any raises in monthly rental fees which might stem from inflation or mismanagement.

These two elements are also crucial to the rationality of the management. In order to establish a mortgage payment schedule, a resident death rate must be predicted, for only when someone dies (or moves permanently to the infirmary) does an apartment turn over and yield another entrance payment. In game-theoretical terms, the management (as one player) bets that any individuals entering Glen Brae (as other players in this retirement-community game) will die according to a predicted rate. Having recruited a population to the community with finite financial resources, the management also bets that the operational costs of maintaining community services will not be inflated to an extent that residents cannot cover them with their monthly rental fees.

These two elements, prediction of life-expectancy and estimation of operating costs, are common to both parties, and establish entry to Glen Brae as a game-like situation. Both players, residents and management, have demonstrated gross departures from pure rationality on both elements.

Management established a 25-year mortgage schedule on the basis of a predicted death rate calculated by the insurance company which holds the mortgage from mortality tables on its insurance policy holders. This estimate was overly "optimistic," as residents did not die as quickly or as frequently as predicted. During the first full year of operation, management predicted that apartment turnover due to death would yield $250,000; actual turnover yielded only $79,000. An administration committee investigating the consequent financial crisis frankly stated:

> One of the problems . . . accrues from the fact that residents are outliving the insurance company statistics for life expectancy . . . . Actual deaths have run about 60% of the actuarily expected rate.

Management had defined the situation as, in game-theory terms, a "game against nature" (Williams, 1966:13, Burger and Freund, 1963:68-69). In such games one plays the odds against a non-thinking, non-strategic other, in this case against a statistical death rate. But this game is in fact a two-person mixed motive game (Schelling, 1960:100), with each party acting strategically, and rationality necessitates a taking into account of the other. In establishing a new prediction of death rate to accompany a shift from a 25- to a 30-year mortgage, the insurance company recognized that:

> **. . . the occupants would probably exercise selection similar to that of purchasers of annuities. That is to say, an individual or couple in ill health would probably not pay the relatively large sum required as (an entrance fee) since there would be no refund in the event of their early death (Internal management document).**

A purchaser of an annuity is an investor, different from the typical purchaser of an insurance policy. He expects to live long enough to realize a return on his investment and is thus probably healthier than the average person his age. Further, in order to make an investment on this large a scale, he is likely to have been so economically privileged as to have received better than average health care. Management erred in not considering the decision of an individual to move to Glen Brae as a strategic decision which would disconfirm the prediction of death rate. I suspect this error was compounded by a failure to recognize that in the case of a couple, the apartment, as specified in the resident's contract, reverts upon the death of one member not to the Corporation, but to the surviving spouse.

For their part, the residents, faced with the more complicated necessity of predicting a life expectancy long enough but not too long, have frequently erred as well. Their judgments of life-expectancy are based on age and perceived health, but also inordinately on the age to which their parents lived, making little allowance for the greater life-expectancy of each successive generation (treated in detail in Marshall, 1972). The words of one resident recognized the typical error of most: "I've lived beyond the time I thought I would."

The second common element in this retirement-community game is the prediction of inflationary effects on the monthly rental fees. Residents assumed the administration would provide an efficient and careful management, holding rental fees as low as possible given inflation. Undoubtedly few residents anticipated inflation would be as great as it has been. In any case, the effects of inflation were compounded by two errors on the part of management. The community was built on the basis of an *unwritten* agreement that it would not be taxed by the locality. Glen Brae is now taxed, and the additional operating expenses have been thrown back at the residents in the form of increased rental payments. Secondly, the costs of medical care were severely underestimated, and the proportion of the monthly rental fee devoted to the provision of medical care has increased more than three-fold in a five-year period. Since high-quality medical care presumably both costs a great deal and prolongs life, this conflict of interest situation represents a two-fold financial threat to the corporation which runs Glen Brae, increasing outflow and holding back inflow. As one resident put it,

> . . . I've heard you get such beautiful care here you haven't a chance of dying. Here is the administration wanting you to die because they want to sell apartments, and the medical staff wanting you to live.

Monthly rental payments have increased at a rate of 18.6% a year over a five-year period; this is an increase which could not have been foreseen by the most intendedly rational person deciding to move to Glen Brae.

In a "mixed-motive" game, neither player can win unless he behaves as the other expects him to do (Schelling, 1960:100). Neither of the players has acted according to the expectations of the other, and there have been many losers. At a mundane level, for many residents it means what is expressed in this statement of a spinster over eighty:

> I just got my bank statement, and it isn't too high. I'll have to be careful from now on. If you knew how long you had (to live) you could figure it out to the cent. But you can't.

Or, as another said:

> I think with the rapid increase in rates here that there are people in great anguish that they will not die until they've spent everything they've got–you see if you could just make it come out even it would be very nice.

Many of the residents have had to leave Glen Brae. Others have found it as difficult to leave as to remain. A discerning resident describes this entrapment as follows:

> There is a terrible feeling amongst the residents that we are caught. It was a great decision–physically and emotionally–to come. We got rid of many possessions, and paid our fees. Now if we've been here five years we haven't much strength. There's that awful feeling of having been caught.

The administration as the other player has lost as well. Glen Brae was established by a Church on a non-profit basis, as a ministry to a segment of the aged population. An administration statement of philosophy notes that

> It was realized that the middle income elderly have great needs just as those who are less affluent–needs of companionship–medical care and freedom from worry.

In terms of freedom from worry, this experiment has failed.

It should be clear that game-theory, with its assumptions of full rationality on the part of both players, does not describe what has actually happened at Glen Brae. What then is its value? Game theory (Luce and Raiffa, 1957:49)

> . . . can be used normatively to tell a person that this is the knowledge he should acquire, and, once he has it, the theory establishes the decisions he should make in order to achieve specified ends.

In its normative function, game theory provides a strong suggestion that one try one's best to take the perspective of the other, and that failure to do so leads to a failure to maximize or satisfy utility. These imperatives to gaining full knowledge and taking the perspective of the other apply to other gerontological situations as well. I cannot extensively delve into these here, but would suggest its applicability to the understanding of failures in retirement planning along several dimensions. What intendedly rational person in planning for his later years could have successfully predicted inflation in property taxes and costs of medical care? Was not a person who planned, thirty years ago, on being cared for by his children in his old age as rational as he might have been, even though he is now caught by a shift in the expectations regarding the flow of services between the generations (Moore, 1966)? I think game-theory leads us to recognize that retirement planning in its immediate and long-range aspects is not likely to be characterized by high levels of rationality. This recognition should be helpful in directing us to policy implications. As the game-theorist Anatol Rapoport suggests (1966:214):

> Rational analysis, for all its inadequacy, is indeed the best instrument of cognition we have. But it is often at its best when it reveals to us the nature of the situation we find ourselves in, even though it may have nothing to tell us how we ought to behave in this situation. . . . Game-theoretical analysis, if pursued to its completion, *perforce* leads us to consider other than strategic modes of thought.

REFERENCES

American Behavioral Scientist. Behavioral Research Council Bulletin, A Current Appraisal of the Behavioral Sciences, March 1964, Sect. 7, Vol. 7.

Burger, E., and Freund J. *Introduction to the Theory of Games*. Englewood Cliffs: Prentice-Hall, 1963.

Boguslaw, R. *The New Utopians*. Englewood Cliffs: Prentice-Hall, 1965.

Goffman, E. *Strategic Interaction*. Oxford: Basil Blackwell, 1970.

Luce, R. Duncan, and H. Raiffa. *Games and Decisions*. New York: John Wiley and Sons, 1957.

Lyman, S., and M. Scott. *A Sociology of the Absurd*. New York: Appleton-Century-Crofts, 1970.

March, J., and Simon, H. *Organizations*. New York: John Wiley and Sons, 1958.

Marshall, Victor W. Continued Living and Dying as Problematical Aspects of Old Age. Unpublished Doctoral Dissertation, Department of Sociology, Princeton University, 1972.

Moore, Omar K., and Anderson, A. R. The Structure of Personality. In O. J. Harvey (Ed.), *Motivation and Social Interaction*. New York: The Ronald Press, 1963, pp. 167-186.

Moore, Wilbert E. Aging and the social system. In John C. McKinney and Frank T. DeVyver (Eds.), *Aging and Social Policy*. New York: Appleton-Century-Crofts, 1966, p. 23-41.

Morgan, James N. Planning for the future and living with risk. *American Behavioral Scientist,* 1963, 40 (May:52-54.

Ofshe, L., and Ofshe, R. *Utility and Choice in Social Interaction.* Englewood Cliffs: Prentice-Hall, 1970.

Rapoport, Anantol. Critiques of game theory. *Behavioral Science,* 1959, 4, 49-66.

Rapoport, Anantol. *Fights, Games, and Debates.* Ann Arbor: The University of Michigan Press, 1960.

Rapoport, Anantol. Two-Person Game Theory. *The Essential Ideas.* Ann Arbor: The University of Michigan Press, 1966.

Schelling, Thomas C. *The Strategy of Conflict.* Oxford: Oxford University Press, 1960.

Schutz, Alfred. Common-sense and scientific interpretation of human action. *Philosophy and Phenomenological Research,* 1953, 14:1-37.

Simon, Herbert. *Models of Man.* New York: John Wiley and Sons, 1957.

Williams, J. O. *The Compleat Strategyst.* New York: McGraw-Hill, 1966.